DINING

in Paradise

NG
in Paradise

A food lover's dream of family style dining in The Bahamas.

RAQUEL FOX

whitecap

Library and Archives Canada Cataloguing in Publication

Fox, Raquel, author
Dining in paradise : a food lover's dream of family style
dining in the Bahamas / Raquel Fox. -- First edition.

Includes index.
ISBN 978-1-77050-320-5 (softcover)

1. Cooking, Bahamian. 2. Cookbooks. I. Title.

TX716.B24F69 2018   641.597296   C2018-904071-8

We acknowledge the financial support of the Government of Canada
through the Canada Book Fund (CBF) for our publishing activities and the
Province of British Columbia through the Book Publishing Tax Credit.

We acknowledge the financial support of the Government of Canada. | **Canada**
Nous reconnaissons l'appui financier du gouvernement du Canada.

1 2 3 4 5   22 21 20 19 18

Printed in Canada by Copywell

DESIGN: KERRY DESIGNS
FOOD PHOTOGRAPHY: MIKE MCCOLL
FOOD STYLIST: GINA ST. GERMAINE
PROOFREADER: PATRICK GERAGHTY

I dedicate this book to two phenomenal women who have impacted my heart and will forever remain in my psyche. My dear grandmother, Mary Campbell, was a humanitarian who fed the neighborhood. As a matter-of-fact, she also fed the elementary school bullies by supplying me with extra portions of her scrumptious homemade lunches. It was her perception of supply and demand.

Althea Fox or Vangie (my beautiful mother-in-law) expressed her opulence of love in every meal she prepared. She taught me how to entertain as if my guests were royalty. My fondest memories will always be family vacations where her preference was to stay at beachfront villas or townhouses, which then enabled us to do what we enjoyed the most, spending quality time with family and cooking! Together we have created many exceptional meals and I will forever be inspired by her love for humanity.

THE ISLANDS OF THE
bahamas

Grand Bahama

Abacos

Berry Islands

Miami

Eleuthera & Harbour
Island

Bimini

Nassau & Paradise
Island

Cat Island

San Salvador

Andros

Rum Cay

Exumas

Long Island

Acklins & Crooked Island

Mayaguana

Ragged Island

Inagua

CONTENTS

A BRIEF HISTORY
of Bahamian Cuisine

The cuisine of The Bahamas reflects a diverse history of influences that shaped our culture and heritage. African, British, French, Spanish, Latin American, Caribbean and Southern U.S cooking methods and flavors are all represented in Bahamian food.

The first inhabitants were the Lucayans, who arrived between 500–800 A.D. They were direct descendants of South America. Their main diet comprised of mostly seafood such as fish, lobster, crab, shrimp and conch. Conch salad is a perfect representation of Latin American cuisine, combining typical flavors of onions, tomatoes, citrus and chilies.

In 1492, Christopher Columbus landed in The Bahamas, introducing the islands to the "New World." Although many attempts were made to colonize the region, a permanent settlement was not established until 1648 when the Puritans, along with other Europeans, settled on the island of Eleuthera. Our national dessert, Guava Duff, was most likely inherited from the English method of steaming dough, as with their traditional Figgy Pudding recipe that dates back to the 16th century.

After the American Revolution, in 1783, the Loyalists were exiled and settled in The Bahamas, bringing with them hundreds of African slaves well versed in the American cuisine of the south. Johnny cake, the Bahamian version of cornbread—along with macaroni and cheese, grits and fried chicken—exemplifies this influence. Fried whole snappers, sauces, and stews made with chopped pieces of bone in the meats, all derive from African methods of cooking that are now popular in Bahamian cuisine.

The Bahamas emerged into the mass tourism industry during the late 1950s and since then has showcased its cuisine to the world. Evolutions and new fusions have captivated my palate and driven my passion to catalogue this historical cuisine passed down to me through my ancestors.

Why This Particular Book

The 700 islands of The Bahamas are scattered across 100,000 square miles of a large archipelago in the southwest Atlantic Ocean. However, only 30 of the islands are inhabited. We welcome over five million visitors every year who are mesmerized by our beautiful white sandy beaches, tropical landscapes and an enticing cuisine that encompasses a rich, flavorful history of our ancestors.

Bahamian cuisine is never bland. Our food consists of a variety of fresh tropical fruits, spices, chilies, lime and rum. Seafood is the staple diet and we believe that fresh is best! As a matter-of-fact, you may venture out to the local dock below the Paradise Island Bridge at Potter's Cay, where you will have the option to select live seafood for the vendor to prepare a mouthwatering native delicacy. Chicken, pork, mutton and beef are prepared with the flavorful and colorful ingredients of the islands. Our cuisine is reminiscent of a tropical paradise—like the islands themselves.

My passion for home-cooked meals was inspired by my grandmother Mary Campbell, who expressed her love for her family through the dishes that she prepared daily. Fortunately, I never craved fast food as a child because our food was more appealing to me than any television fast-food advertisement could be. While being raised by my dear grandmother, I was fortunate to be the heir of three generations of family recipes.

These quintessential treasures have become one of my family's most sacred jewels, and now I'm sharing them with you.

This book is filled with exotic and easy-to-make cuisines mainly from The Bahamas along with my favorite recipes from a few of the other Caribbean Islands. It's for people who live to eat exceptionally.

Come with me as I take you on a journey of the senses. Imagine the fresh ocean breeze as you place your feet on the most impeccable white sandy beaches and dine on fresh seafood with exotic flavors that you can only experience in island-style cooking. As we say in the Bahamas, "If you're going, let's go!"

— Raquel Fox

INTRO*duction*

There's an aura that is so profound about Sundays in The Bahamas. It's an atmosphere of tranquility and a celebration of life. Friends and family gather to dine together as they exchange love, laughter and spirituality. At the end of the evening every person leaves feeling sated with a zeal for life. Our family's dining table was regularly extended as family members brought friends, and friends invited other friends, so that by the end of the day it was a party in the backyard!

I was amazed at how the older men made rhythmic sounds with a saw, scrub board and goat skin drum (called Rake-and-Scrape music). They enjoyed a game of dominoes under the massive tamarind tree while sipping on ice-cold beers or rum cocktails. The women danced, played cards and told stories as the kids played hop-scotch and hide-and-seek.

In my family, my grandmother proclaimed Wednesdays "soup days." These soups were cooked long and slow and were a true labor of love. The scent of freshly baked breads infused with the aroma from the soup lingered throughout the neighborhood—I looked forward to the alluring perfume every week while walking home from school. Our native soups are filled with a variety of protein, vegetables and spices.

My grandmother always cooked enough food for a crowd. She never turned away an uninvited guest or a hungry neighbor who followed the trail of enticing aromas to our house. Cooking was her Zen, sanctuary and passion. I'm proud to say that it was passed down the lineage to me.

This cookbook is my way of sharing my heritage, love and passion for Bahamian cuisine. It encompasses the culture, authentic flavors and spices that originate from our many beautiful islands.

When I made this decision to document my heritage, I did not want to write just another Caribbean-style cookbook with the same recipes that have already been popularized, but alternatively my goal was to appeal to epicureans like myself who are always searching for new, interesting and exceptional flavors.

As a chef and instructor at George Brown College in Toronto, one of the most common questions asked by my students is, "What is Bahamian Cuisine and how does it differ from other Caribbean cuisines?" Bahamian cuisine happens to be one of the most flavorful and unique cooking styles throughout the Caribbean, although it remains still undiscovered by many in the outside world. *Dining in Paradise* is my quest to offer more exposure to our food and culture, and to the history of our islands.

One of my true joys in life is travelling the

world and meeting people, learning about their culture and sharing mine with them. One of my most memorable excursions was in Switzerland on my honeymoon in 1994, where I was drawn to the sweet and smoky aromas drifting from Mount Rigi. I was compelled to ascend the mountain in a cable car where my husband and I discovered breathtaking scenery of beautiful summer homes, wildflowers and a massive barbecue filled with a variety of homemade sausages and bratwurst. We were invited over by friendly smiling faces, and as I took a seat at their table we realized that we had a temporary barrier — language. It didn't matter in the least, as they searched for the expression on my face while loading my plate with food. There was silence as I closed my eyes and savored the most flavorful bratwurst, sausages and homemade breads. I gave a thumb's up and they responded with a celebratory outburst! I sampled the different flavors of beers, and we danced.

I showed my gratitude by contributing my family's potato salad to the already opulent spread. They enjoyed it immensely. The women observed and wrote down the recipe while paying special attention to the details. Someone brought a map and I knew immediately that they were inquiring about our origin. The excitement in their inquisitive eyes reflected a thousand words, so I drew a sketch of coconut trees, sandy beaches and seafood on the grill, while my husband pointed out the location of The Bahamas on the map. They were certainly intrigued, as each person pointed to themselves, then the map, acknowledging that they would visit

The Bahamas eventually. I gave a thumb's up with a warm smile, waved goodbye and then raced to catch the last cable car that was heading down the mountain. What a spectacular day!

I've had so many amazing cultural experiences during my travels, but the most meaningful memories for me came from dining with the natives of the places I visit (though I also appreciate the luxury of fine dining at Michelin star restaurants—a hobby of mine).

Dining in Paradise is a document of my family's recipes, and much more. I'm the type of chef who has always pushed the boundaries. I enjoy fusion, as there are so many similarities between cultures, as well as differences to respect and celebrate in each other's heritage. The chef in me enjoys exploring with many of our native ingredients but I'm not intimidated when infusing new flavors (which accounts for creating some astounding recipes).

I was told by other authors that your first book is special because it speaks your truth and is not inhibited or influenced by the opinion of others; this is true for me, as I am confident that I was born to write this book and share it with the world. I believe in a quote from my favorite essayist, Ralph Waldo Emerson, "Once you make a decision, the universe conspires to make it happen."

I'm thankful for the televised cooking shows that encourage people to try a variety of cuisines, that pique their interest to travel to these destinations and that, most of all, get them cooking!

Seasonal MENUS

MENUS FOR SPRING

Easter Brunch

I'm particularly fond of spring as it brings forth the most picturesque gardens just in time for my family's traditional Easter Sunday Brunch. Some Bahamians attend an early church service, then dine at one of the local hotel's restaurants for an extravagant spread. I prefer the intricacies of entertaining and dining at home.

Vivacious Sunrise
Sweet Potato Spring Frittata
Soursop Pancakes with Honey-Thyme Syrup
Ragged Island Stew Fish
Andros Native Grits
Tropical Mango Cheesecake with Sea Grape Pearls

Family Islands Regatta Party

The National Family Island Regatta is reminiscent of an extended family reunion beach party. Although many of the out-islands host their own regattas during the spring and summer months, most visitors and Bahamians gather in George Town's Elizabeth Harbour (during the last full week in April), to enjoy five days of sloop sailing competition in customized wooden boats. On shore, the festivities continue with live music, art exhibits, beauty pageants and an ambrosial selection of scrumptious Bahamian cuisine prepared by local vendors.

Pigeon Peas & Dumpling Soup
My Bahamian Conch Fritters with
GoomBay Sauce
Androsian Stuffed Crabs
Curry Mutton with Coconut Milk
Exuma Cracked Conch
Exotic Cole Slaw
Steamed Coconut Jasmine Rice
Peas & Rice with Coconut Oil
Twice Fried Plantains
Eleuthera Pineapple Tart with Pistachio Butter

MENUS FOR SUMMER

Picnics & Barbecues

It's time to fire up the grill and enjoy "entertaining in the great outdoors." During the summer, I usually prepare most of the foods indoors, finish on the grill and serve guests immediately. It's important to practise food safety by keeping foods that should be kept cold (salads, meat, etc.) in the refrigerator or coolers equipped with ice to maintain a temperature of 4°C (39°F) or lower. Impress your guests with this crowd-pleasing summer barbecue.

Native Skillet Cornbread
Vangie's Delicious Layered Salad
Bahama Grilled Grouper in Parchment
Guava Barbecue Beef Ribs
Tangy Macaroni Salad
Roasted Corn with Maple-Chile Dressing
Coconut Custard Pie

Independence Day Celebration

When I think of my country's independence two things come to mind, the date that The Bahamas gained its independence (July 10, 1973), and spending quality time with my loved ones. Celebrate your country's Independence by entertaining with a sensational breakfast and dinner.

Breakfast Menu

Independence Morning Fruitty-Puffed Pancake

Aunt Tia's Coconut Johnny Cake

Boil Fish & Taittinger

Dinner Menu

Grand Bahama Conch Chowder with Kaffir Lime Essence

Spinach, Hibiscus & Crabapple Salad with Creamy

Soursop-Peppercorn Dressing

Bahama Rock Minced Lobster

Nassau Grouper Fingers

Curried Rice

Switcha Root Vegetables

Petit Guava Duff

MENUS FOR AUTUMN

Cocktails & Appetizers Event

Autumn is the most pleasant season in The Bahamas. The weather is sunny during the daytime with breezy evenings, therefore spectacular fruity cocktails are enjoyed throughout the season. It's the perfect time of year to celebrate life with a fabulous cocktail and appetizer party.

Yellow Bird

Goombay Smash

Sky Juice

Tropical Fruit Cheese Log

Tamarind Chickpea Dip with Mamey Crema

Abaco Stone Crabs with Lemongrass

& Dill Dipping Sauce

Harbour Island Lobster Salad in Campari Cups

Island Crab Cakes Wrapped in Seaweed

Konky Conch Cakes

Tropical Mango Shrimp on Lemongrass Skewers

Savory Lamb Turnovers

Pear-a-dise Thin Crust Pizza with Smoked Duck

& Goat Cheese Crumble

Chocolate Coconut Purses with Banana Caramel

Thanksgiving Feast

Bahamian Thanksgiving is called Harvest Thanksgiving. It's associated with biblical beliefs of providing a bountiful feast to celebrate the first fruits of the harvest. It is said that earlier Bahamian farmers provided sheep and goat meat as the main dish on their tables, as turkey was, and still is, imported. My family's Thanksgiving feast is legendary, and I'm excited to be sharing it with you.

Harvest Pumpkin Soup

Native Corn & Charred Pepper Salad

Aunt Tia's Festive Holiday Ham

Fennel Spiced Oven-Fried Turkey

Hickory Smoked Bacon Stuffing

Cranberry Citrus Sauce

Sweet Potato Mash

Home-Style Peppercorn Gravy

Sautéed Callaloo

Mad Mac & Cheese

Sapodilla Spiced Cake with Dilly Cream

Menus For Winter
Traditional Christmas Dinner

There's nothing that says home like an exceptional Christmas Dinner. It should be warm and inviting with the perfect holiday ambiance and nuances of spice and citrus. Forget the eggnog this year and enjoy a Bahamian Soupsop Punch drink.

Soupsop Punch
Vangie's Broccoflower Salad
Exotic Coleslaw
Citrus Glazed Stuffed Cornish Hens
Aunt Tia's Festive Holiday Ham
Peas & Rice with Coconut Oil
Twice Fried Plantains
Lady Pat's Award-Winning Potato Salad
Caribbean Bread Pudding with Ginger Cooked Cream

New Years Eve Dinner

Chill the champagne, bring out the china and polish the silverware for an unforgettable candlelight New Years Eve dinner. It's the time to reflect over the year, toast to a prosperous future with friends and indulge with warm exotic soufflés while watching the firework show.

Savory Coconut Curry Soup
Drum "Beet" Salad
Creamy Rock Lobster Mac 'n' Cheese
Long Island Braised Duck in Guava Rum Sauce
Fennel Spiced Cabbage
Roasted Sage & Garlic Mashed Cassavas
Exotic Soufflés

Androsia Batik Factory, Andros Island
Handmade Batik established by the Birch
family in 1973

WEEKEND BAHAMIAN BRUNCH

Andros Native Grit

Aunt Tia's Coconut Johnnycake

Cat Island Potato Bread

Eleuthera Native Fruit Salad

Nassau Chicken Souse

Bahamian Pepper Sauce

Exuma Stew Conch

Corned Beef & Eggs.

BIOGRAPHICAL
Profile

Raquel Fox is a professional chef and motivational speaker. She grew up in The Bahamas and spent a great deal of time in the kitchen as a young girl. She was lucky to have the secrets of preparing conch, spiny lobsters, chowders, johnny cakes, mutton, oxtail, cassava and other traditional Bahamian specialties handed down to her while living and cooking with her grandmother. Although Raquel acquired a lifelong interest in global multicultural cuisines while attending international schools, her heart is in the Bahamian kitchen.

Raquel took her passion into the professional kitchen while still in The Bahamas with her husband. She began organizing "wine-and-dine" events at a number of prestigious venues including The Lyford Cay and Old Fort Bay Club: two of The Bahamas' most revered kitchens. Based on her success during these events, Raquel and her husband opened a fine dining restaurant, The Wine Lounge, voted on USA Today's list one of the 10 best lounges in the Bahamas, where they celebrated many successful years before wanderlust led them to think about, and eventually relocate, to Canada.

Deciding to hone her craft by attending culinary school, Raquel chose The Chef School at George Brown College in Toronto, as it was the best place to explore all aspects of cooking,

food culture, and international cuisine. She is also an alumni and an instructor for the continuing education course at the college for her Caribbean Cooking Class.

*Acknowledg*MENTS

A cookbook is a chef's memoir brought to life by zealous artists and enthusiastic friends. I would like to extend my gratitude to Nick Rundall and The Whitecap Family for believing in my concept and turning this dream into a reality.

Many thanks to Mike McColl, an exceptional food photographer who captured the essence of Bahamian cuisine and culture in his photographs. Thanks to Gina St. Germaine, celebrity food stylist who worked meticulously while opening her treasure chest of props and accessories to captivate the reader's curiosity.

I greatly appreciate my George Brown College Family, Tony Garcia, Signe Sohrbeck, and Chef Ryan Whibbs PhD, RSE for your support and encouragement. Thanks to Ken Peters, my original proofreader and Carol Sherman, my editor.

Thank you to Cookbook Authors Nettie Cronish and Naomi Duguid for such heartfelt quotes. Nettie, thanks for being my number one cheerleader and friend.

Bahamian cuisine, music and culture goes hand in hand, so much thanks to John Zonnicle and The Bahamas Junkanoo Legends for participating in the Appetizer Event & Photography for the cookbook. Thanks to Facinie for the lovely hats and fascinators for The Tea Party Photography. The readers will experience A Taste of The Bahamas through your efforts.

Thanks to The Bahamas Ministry of Tourism, Toronto, Ontario for the picturesque cultural photographs of our beautiful Islands.

A warm thank you to my friends Courtney and Adele for graciously inviting my "dream team" (Mike, Gina & Kerry Plumley), into their beautiful home to capture some amazing photographs. I couldn't work tirelessly on the recipes without my Queens, Giovanna, Alana and my aunt Tia who were my faithful assistants and recipe testers throughout this process.

Drum roll and thank you to my wonderful husband, Ruben and sons, Ruben Jr. and Rashad who held the fort down, while I poured my heart into this cookbook. One down, six more to go.

The local Fish Fry, Arawak Cay,
Nassau Bahamas

The Straw Market
Nassau, Paradise Island

CHAPTER 1

RAQUEL'S *Private Stash*

Become familiar with my most sacred jewels of seasonings, sauces, chutneys and jams. Condiments are the key to complementing and elevating your favorite salads, soups, sandwiches and more, so be inspired and get cooking!

- RAQUEL'S SEASONED SALT
- BAHAMA FISH SEASONING
- BAHAMIAN PEPPER SAUCE
- CUMIN CRÈME
- MINT CRÈME
- GREEN VINAIGRETTE
- SWEET PEPPERY TARTAR SAUCE
- RAQUEL'S GOOMBAY SAUCE
- GREEN COCKTAIL SAUCE
- GREEN MANGO CHUTNEY
- LEMONGRASS & DILL DIPPING SAUCE
- CURRY OIL
- ISLAND CURRANT KETCHUP
- HOMEMADE TOMATO SAUCE
- CARIBBEAN MANGO SALSA
- TAMARIND CHUTNEY
- GUAVA BELL PEPPER JAM
- MANGO PASSION VINAIGRETTE
- CREAMY SOURSOP PEPPERCORN DRESSING
- BALSAMIC PLATE
- TAMARIND GLAZE & GRILLING SAUCE
- MUSTARD & CHILI LIME MAYONNAISE
- HERBED JOHNNY CAKE CROUTONS
- GINGER COOKED CREAM
- SEA GRAPE PEARLS
- HOMEMADE DUMPLINGS
- EXOTIC CHIPS
- HOME STYLE PEPPERCORN GRAVY
- CITRUS CRANBERRY SAUCE
- DULCE DE LECHE SAUCE
- TENDERIZING CONCHS

Raquel's Seasoned Salt

This salt is the ultimate flavor enhancer for vegetables, poultry, meat and seafood. Triple the recipe and store in an airtight container for convenience.

Makes 1/3 cup (80 mL)

1. Place all ingredients in a small dish and mix thoroughly with a fork. Keep in an airtight container.

INGREDIENTS

2 Tbsp (30 mL) fine sea salt
1 Tbsp (15 mL) garlic powder
1 tsp (5 mL) onion powder
1/2 tsp (2 mL) ground cumin
1 tsp (5 mL) smoked paprika

Bahama Fish Seasoning

Here's a recipe for the traditional method of seasoning fish in the Bahamas.

Makes 3 Tbsp (45 mL)

1. Place salt and pepper on a cutting board. Use the blade of a knife and mince together.
2. Store in an airtight container for up to 2 weeks.

INGREDIENTS

2 Tbsp (30 mL) sea salt
1/2 Scotch bonnet or habanero pepper, finely diced (using food safety gloves)

Bahamian Pepper Sauce

This sauce is an essential ingredient to enhance the flavor of souses, soups and stews.

Makes 1 cup (250 mL)

INGREDIENTS

2 Scotch bonnet peppers, finely diced
1/2 tsp (2 mL) fine sea salt
Juice of 8 limes

1. Place salt and pepper on a cutting board. Use the blade of a knife and mince together. Place pepper mixture and lime juice in a small sterilized jar and shake well.
2. Let steep for 30 minutes. Keep in the refrigerator for up to 2 weeks.

Cumin Crème

Use this crème as a garnish for curry and soup dishes.

Makes 1 cup (250 mL)

INGREDIENTS

1 tsp (5 mL) cumin seeds
1 cup (250 mL) sour cream

1. In a small skillet over medium heat, toast cumin seeds until fragrant, about 1–2 minutes. Transfer to a small plate to cool.
2. Grind the seeds in a spice or coffee grinder. Place sour cream in a small bowl and fold in cumin. Cover and refrigerate for up to 1 week.

Garlic Oil

INGREDIENTS

1 head roasted garlic
2 cups (500 mL) olive oil

1. To prepare the garlic oil, remove cloves from head of garlic. In a 1-quart (1 L) saucepan, add cloves and oil and simmer over low heat until cloves are light brown. Transfer to a small dish. (Save the flavorful garlic for another recipe.) Set aside and reserve the fragrant garlic oil.

Mint Crème

Enhance desserts with this minty garnish.

Makes 2 cups (500 mL)

1. Whisk cream and sugar in a medium bowl to stiff peaks. Add mint leaves and fold. Set aside in a small dish covered with plastic wrap and keep in the refrigerator. Serve as a topping for desserts and soups.

   VARIATION: Replace 35% cream with 2 cups (500 mL) plain Greek yogurt as a savory garnish to enhance appetizers and soups.

INGREDIENTS

2 cups (500 mL) whipping (or heavy) cream (35%)

1 tsp (5 mL) confectioner's (icing) sugar

4 mint leaves, chiffonade

Green Vinaigrette

This vinaigrette with nuances of mint is a perfect enhancer for salads, appetizers, soups and rice.

Makes 1 cup (250 mL)

1. In the bowl of a food processor, combine all ingredients (except oil, salt and pepper) and purée.
2. Gradually add oil, then add a pinch of salt and pepper to taste.

INGREDIENTS

1/4 bunch chives

1 Tbsp (15 mL) chopped Italian parsley leaves

1 tsp (5 mL) fresh thyme leaves

1/4 bunch fresh chadon beni (see page 220)

2 cloves garlic, smashed

1/3 cup (80 mL) red wine vinegar

1/2 cup (125 mL) extra virgin olive oil

Pinch of salt

Freshly ground black pepper

Sweet Peppery Tartar Sauce

This sauce is a perfect accompaniment to seafood.

Makes 1 1/2 cups (375 mL)

1. In the bowl of a food processor with the machine running, place egg yolks. Gradually add lemon juice, mustard and bell pepper until combined. Slowly add oil to make the mayonnaise.
2. Transfer to a small bowl, fold in relish, hot pepper (with seeds), and season to taste with salt.
3. Cover bowl with plastic wrap and chill in the refrigerator until ready to serve. Because there are egg yolks in this recipe, the sauce does not store well. Make fresh and use it right away.
4.

   CAUTION: This recipe contains raw egg yolks. If you are concerned about the safety of using raw eggs, use pasteurized eggs in the shell or 1/4 cup (60 mL) pasteurized liquid whole eggs.

INGREDIENTS

2 large egg yolks (see Caution)
2 tsp (10 mL) lemon juice
1 tsp (5 mL) Dijon mustard
1/4 piece roasted red bell pepper
1 cup (250 mL) extra virgin olive oil
1/4 cup (60 mL) sweet relish
1 hot cherry pepper, diced
Raquel's Seasoned Salt to taste (see recipe, page 2)

Raquel's GoomBay Sauce

GoomBay Summers is the name of my catering company. The name pays homage to this vibrant festival that I enjoyed immensely in my youth. This sauce is simply extraordinary as a dipping sauce for seafood and fries, or as a spread for sandwiches.

Makes 1 1/2 cups (375 mL)

1. Place all ingredients in a small bowl and mix well. Store in the refrigerator for up to 1 week.

INGREDIENTS

1 cup (250 mL) mayonnaise
1 tsp (5 mL) Dijon mustard
1 Tbsp (15 mL) sambal oelek (chili paste)
1 Tbsp (15 mL) fish sauce
Juice of 1/2 lime
1 Tbsp (15 mL) light brown sugar
1 fresh mint leaf, diced
1/2 tsp (2 mL) diced fresh dill
1 fresh basil leaf, diced
1 tsp (5 mL) ketchup

Green Cocktail Sauce

This sauce is a great complement to seafood or use as a dip or garnish.

Makes 2 cups (500 mL)

1. In a small saucepan, add vinegar, apple and tomato over medium heat and cook for 5 minutes.
2. Transfer to the bowl of a food processor and pulse a few times for a coarse consistency. Place in a small bowl, then mix in remaining ingredients and season to taste.

INGREDIENTS

1/2 cup (125 mL) rice wine vinegar (mirin)
1 medium Granny Smith apple, peeled and diced
1 large green heirloom tomato, peeled and diced with seeds removed
1 shallot, diced
1 tsp (5 mL) minced garlic
1 tsp (5 mL) fresh grated horseradish
Salt to taste

Green Mango Chutney

Serve this chutney as an accompaniment to curry dishes and stews.

Makes 2 cups (500 mL)

1. Peel and dice mangoes and transfer to the bowl of a food processor. Add onion and tomatoes and purée.
2. In a small saucepan, add mango mixture over medium heat. Add remaining ingredients (except for vinegar) and cook for 30 minutes.
3. Add vinegar and simmer for 15 minutes. Transfer to sterilized jars and store in the refrigerator for up to 3 weeks.

INGREDIENTS

2 whole green mangoes, peeled and diced
1/2 cup (125 mL) roughly chopped onion
1 green tomato, seeded and diced
1/2 cup (125 mL) golden raisins
1/2 cup (125 mL) lightly packed brown sugar
4 cloves
1 Scotch bonnet pepper, finely diced
1/4 cup (60 mL) white vinegar

Lemongrass & Dill Dipping Sauce

This dipping sauce is a great accompaniment to seafood.

Makes 1 1/4 cups (310 mL)

1. Place all ingredients in a small glass dish and mix well. Adjust seasoning to taste.

INGREDIENTS

1 Tbsp (15 mL) lemongrass paste
  or purée
1 tsp (5 mL) minced ginger
1 tsp (5 mL) roasted garlic purée
1 cup (250 mL) mayonnaise
2 tsp (10 mL) Dijon mustard
1 Tbsp (15 mL) fresh lemon juice
1 tsp (5 mL) light brown sugar
1 tsp (5 mL) chili paste
1 Tbsp (15 mL) fresh dill

Curry Oil

This oil is a great way to spice up your favorite dishes.

Makes 1 cup (250 mL)

1. In a small saucepan, heat 2 Tbsp (30 mL) of the oil over medium-low heat. Add curry powder, turmeric, cumin, ginger and thyme and cook until fragrant, about 3 minutes.
2. Add garlic, zest and remaining oil to the pan. Reduce heat to low and cook, about 1–2 minutes. Transfer to a food processor and purée.
3. Pour spiced-oil into a small glass bowl. Let the sediments sink to the bottom.
4. Line a strainer with cheesecloth and strain the oil. Store in an airtight container in a cool dry place for up to a month.

INGREDIENTS

1 1/4 cups (310 mL) grapeseed or
  canola oil, divided
1 Tbsp (15 mL) Caribbean curry powder
1/2 tsp (2 mL) ground turmeric
1/4 tsp (1 mL) ground cumin
1/2 tsp (2 mL) ground ginger
1/2 tsp (2 mL) ground thyme leaves
2 garlic cloves, minced
Zest of 1 lime
1/4 tsp (1 mL) fine sea salt

Island Currant Ketchup

Here's the best-tasting homemade ketchup, with black currant nuances.

Makes 3 cups (750 mL)

1. In a 3-quart (3 L) pot, heat oil over medium heat. Add onion and garlic and cook for 3 minutes.
2. Add tomatoes and jelly and cook, stirring, for 30 minutes. Add remaining ingredients and cook, stirring occasionally, for 15 minutes more. Let cool.
3. Transfer to the bowl of a food processor and purée until smooth. Store in sterilized jars and keep in a cool dry place or the refrigerator for up to 1 month.

INGREDIENTS

3 Tbsp (45 mL) olive oil
1/2 medium onion, diced
4 cloves garlic, diced
4 ripe Roma tomatoes, peeled and diced with seeds removed
1 cup (250 mL) sea grape jelly or jam or black currant jam
1 Tbsp (15 mL) light brown sugar (optional)
1 Tbsp (15 mL) basil leaves, chiffonade
1 tsp (5 mL) ground coriander
2 tsp (10 mL) ground mustard
1 tsp (5 mL) ground allspice
1/2 tsp (2 mL) ground cinnamon
1/4 cup (60 mL) cider vinegar
Fine sea salt and pepper to taste

Homemade Tomato Sauce

This superb tomato sauce takes half the time of most homemade tomato sauces and has a flavor that's unmatched.

Makes 2 cups (500 mL)

1. In a 3-quart (3 L) pot, heat oil over medium heat. Add onion and garlic and cook for 3 minutes.
2. Add tomatoes. Reduce heat and simmer, stirring occasionally, for 30 minutes. Add basil, oregano and salt and cook for 5 minutes more.
3. Using an immersion blender, purée sauce to a smooth consistency. Let cool. Store in sterilized jars and keep in the refrigerator for up to 2 weeks.

INGREDIENTS

3 Tbsp (45 mL) olive oil
1/2 medium onion, diced
4 cloves garlic, diced
4 cups (1 L) diced heirloom tomatoes
2 Tbsp (15 mL) fresh basil, chiffonade
1 tsp (5 mL) dried oregano
Fine sea salt to taste

CARIBBEAN MANGO SALSA

This flavorful salsa has an exotic Caribbean twist.

Makes 6 cups (1.5 L)

1. In the bowl of a food processor, combine tomatoes, onion, green pepper, cilantro, garlic, lime juice and Scotch bonnet pepper and pulse a few times to make a coarse salsa. Season to taste with salt and pepper. Transfer to a medium bowl.
2. Squeeze remaining lime juice over avocado to prevent it from turning brown and add to the bowl.
3. Add remaining ingredients to the bowl and mix well.

INGREDIENTS

2 cups (500 mL) diced tomatoes
1/2 onion, diced
1/4 piece green bell pepper, diced
1/4 bunch cilantro
4 cloves garlic
Juice of 1 1/2 limes, divided
1 green Scotch bonnet pepper, diced
Salt and pepper to taste
1 ripe avocado, diced
2 ripe Kent mangoes, peeled and diced
1 cup (250 mL) diced fresh pineapple
1 cup (250 mL) canned black beans, rinsed
2 Tbsp (30 mL) simple syrup
1/4 tsp (1 mL) ground allspice
1/4 tsp (1 mL) ground cinnamon

TAMARIND CHUTNEY

This chutney is a great accompaniment to curry dishes and some appetizers that may need a little more "oomph."

Makes 3 cups (750 mL)

1. In a 1.5-quart (1.5 L) saucepan, combine paste and water over medium heat. Stir paste while separating with a wooden spoon and bring sauce to a boil. Reduce heat and simmer until sauce thickens slightly to coat the back of a spoon.
2. Remove the pan from heat and strain the sauce into a bowl. Discard the skin and any stray seeds, then return tamarind sauce to pan over medium heat.
3. Add sugar and stir to dissolve. Add remaining ingredients and let simmer, about 20–30 minutes, adjusting with 1/2 cup (125 mL) water if the sauce is too thick.
4. Let cool and store in a sterilized jar or an airtight container in the refrigerator for up to 2 weeks.

INGREDIENTS

2 cups (500 mL) seedless tamarind paste
3 cups (750 mL) water
1/2 cup (125 mL) lightly packed brown sugar
1/2 tsp (2 mL) salt
4 cloves garlic, diced
1/4 cup (60 mL) diced onion
1/4 bunch cilantro, diced
1/2 green Scotch bonnet pepper (optional)

Guava Bell Pepper Jam

This is the tastiest jam to complement any charcuterie board or appetizer. It's exceptional as a glaze over pork, or add it to your favorite barbecue sauce.

Makes 2 cups (500 mL)

1. In a 3-quart (3 L) pot, combine paste and water over medium heat. Break paste into pieces with a wooden spoon and stir to melt into a sauce that coats the back of the spoon (adjust with a little more water, if needed).
2. Add remaining ingredients. Reduce heat and simmer, about 30 minutes.
3. Let cool and store in sterilized jars for up to 3 weeks.

INGREDIENTS

1/2 cup (125 mL) guava paste
3 cups (750 mL) water
1/2 cup (125 mL) diced pink guavas
1/2 red bell pepper, diced
1 tsp (5 mL) ground coriander
1 tsp (5 mL) ground nutmeg
Juice of 1 lemon
2 tsp (10 mL) sambal oelek (chili paste)

Mango Passion Vinaigrette

Here's a taste of The Bahamas. Toss or drizzle this vinaigrette over salads for a citrusy taste with nuances of passion fruit.

Makes 3 3/4 cups (940 mL)

1. In the bowl of a food processor or blender, combine all ingredients (except oil) and purée. While motor is running, slowly pour in olive oil.
2. Season to taste with salt and pepper.
3. Store in sterilized glass jars and refrigerate for up to 2 weeks.

INGREDIENTS

1 cup (250 mL) frozen mango juice concentrate
1 cup (250 mL) frozen orange juice concentrate
1/4 cup (60 mL) frozen lemonade or limeade concentrate
1/4 cup (60 mL) frozen strawberries
1 Tbsp (15 mL) red wine vinegar
2 Tbsp (30 mL) Dijon mustard
1/4 tsp (1 mL) salt + extra to taste
1/4 tsp (1 mL) freshly ground black pepper + extra to taste
1/4 cup (60 mL) extra virgin olive oil

Creamy Soursop Peppercorn Dressing

The exotic flavor of this dressing will impress your guests with its creamy and mellow honeyed flavor.

Makes 1 1/2 cups (375 mL)

1. In the bowl of a food processor, combine all ingredients (except oil) and purée.
2. Season with salt to taste. With the motor running, gradually add oil.
3. Store in a sterilized jar in your refrigerator for up to 2 weeks.

INGREDIENTS

3/4 cup (190 mL) soursop juice or nectar
1/2 cup (125 mL) mayonnaise
1 Tbsp (15 mL) condensed milk
1 tsp (5 mL) granulated sugar (optional)
1 tsp (5 mL) tri-color peppercorns, grounded
1 clove garlic, crushed
1/4 piece small sweet onion, diced
Salt to taste
1/4 cup (60 mL) extra virgin olive oil

Balsamic Sheet

This edible sheet can be cut into any shape that you prefer. Let your imagination go wild. Use to complement salads and appetizers.

Makes 2 cups (500 mL)

1. In a large bowl, cover gelatin sheets with cold water and soak and let bloom until soft.
2. In a 1-quart (1 L) saucepan, whisk together vinegar and agar-agar. Place over high heat and bring to a boil for 3 minutes.
3. Remove from heat. Lightly squeeze water from gelatin sheets and add to the pan. Stir until sheets melt into the liquid.
4. Line 2 baking sheets with sheets of acetate or a nonstick silicon baking mat. Pour vinegar mixture into the pan to a depth of 1/8 inch (3 mm).
5. Refrigerate until set, about 1 hour. Cut into desired shapes.

TIP: Acetate is available at craft or baking shops.

INGREDIENTS

8 gelatin sheets
2 cups (500 mL) balsamic vinegar
1 tsp (5 mL) agar-agar

Tamarind Glaze & Grilling Sauce

This is a real savory flavor enhancer. It's a delicious glaze that complements all foods placed over a hot grill.

Makes 1 1/2 cups (375 mL)

1. In a 1.5-quart (1.5 L) saucepan, combine paste and water over medium heat. Stir paste while separating with a wooden spoon and bring sauce to a boil. Reduce heat and simmer until sauce thickens slightly to coat the back of a spoon.
2. Remove the pan from the heat and strain the sauce into a bowl. Discard the skin and any stray seeds, then return the tamarind sauce to the pan over medium heat.
3. Add remaining ingredients. Reduce heat and simmer, about 20–30 minutes. Store in a sterilized glass jar or an airtight container in the refrigerator for 2 weeks.

INGREDIENTS

1 cup (250 mL) seedless tamarind paste
3 cups (750 mL) water
2/3 cup (160 mL) lightly packed brown sugar
1 tsp (5 mL) minced ginger
1 Tbsp (15 mL) diced fresh tarragon leaves
1 tsp (5 mL) ground cinnamon
1 tsp (5 mL) ground allspice
1/2 tsp (2 mL) ground thyme
1/4 cup (60 mL) rice wine vinegar (mirin)
1 Tbsp (15 mL) sambal oelek (chili paste)
Salt and pepper to taste

Mustard & Chili Lime Mayonnaise

This citrusy mayonnaise is something to savor. Try it on all of your recipes and make this your #1 mayonnaise of choice.

Makes 1 1/4 cups (310 mL)

1. In the bowl of a food processor, combine all ingredients (except oil) and purée. With the motor running, gradually add oil. Taste and adjust seasoning. Because there are egg yolks in this recipe, this sauce does not store well. Make fresh and use it right away.

INGREDIENTS

2 egg yolks (see Caution, page 5)
Juice and zest of 2 limes
1 Tbsp (15 mL) Dijon mustard
1/4 tsp (1 mL) salt
1 tsp (5 mL) sambal oelek (chili paste)
1 Tbsp (15 mL) diced cilantro
1 tsp (5 mL) granulated sugar
Pinch of black pepper
1 cup (250 mL) extra virgin olive oil

Herbed Johnny Cake Croutons

Here's a gift from my family to yours. These desirable croutons or crumble (see Variation) will become your favorite topping for soups, salads and desserts.

Makes 12 cups (2.8 L)

1. Preheat oven to 350°F (180°C). Line a baking sheet with parchment paper and set aside.
2. To prepare the herbed dressing, in a 2-quart (2L) saucepan, heat oil over medium heat. Add remaining ingredients and cook, stirring, for 5 minutes. Remove and discard garlic.
3. Cut johnny cake into 3/4-inch (2 cm) cubes and place in a large bowl. Pour oil over top and toss.
4. Place bread cubes on the baking sheet and bake for 15 minutes for crisp, golden croutons.

VARIATION: For Johnny Cake Crumble, place the croutons in a plastic bag and crush lightly with a mallet.

INGREDIENTS

1 recipe for Aunt Tia's Johnny Cake (see Variation, page 34)

Herbed Dressing

1 cup (250 mL) olive oil
2 garlic cloves, smashed
1 Tbsp (15 mL) diced dried Italian parsley
1 Tbsp (15 mL) diced dried basil
1 tsp (5 mL) salt
1/2 tsp (2 mL) freshly ground black pepper

Ginger Cooked Cream

This gingery cream is as enticing as its name. Enhance the flavor of vanilla cakes by poking holes in the cake with a skewer and pouring the cream over to soak. Serve it on the side to drizzle over bread puddings, pies and even ice cream, so yummy.

Makes 4 cups (1 L)

1. In a 4-quart (4 L) saucepan, pour in beer over medium-high heat and reduce by half. Add cream and reduce heat to medium.
2. Slit vanilla pods in half with a paring knife. Scrape out the seeds and transfer to the cream mixture. Add sugar and continue to cook, stirring occasionally, for 30 minutes until slightly thickened to coat the back of a spoon.
3. Add candied ginger and cook for 5 minutes more.

INGREDIENTS

1/2 cup (125 mL) ginger beer
4 cups (1 L) whipping (or heavy) cream (35%)
2 vanilla bean pods
1/2 cup (125 mL) granulated sugar
1/2 cup (125 mL) diced candied ginger

Sea Grape Pearls

Serve these pearls over ice cream or as an accompaniment to various desserts.

Makes 1/2 cup (125 mL)
Serves 2-4

INGREDIENTS

2 cups (500 mL) vegetable oil
2 gelatin sheets
1/3 cup (80 mL) grape juice, unsweetened (or sea grape juice)
1/4 cup (60 mL) white grape juice
1/2 tsp (2 mL) agar-agar

1. Pour oil into a clear 1-quart (1 L) container. Place in the freezer to chill the oil to a temperature of 35˚F (2˚C).
2. In a large bowl, cover gelatin sheets with cold water and soak and let bloom until soft. Squeeze gently. Set aside.
3. In a small bowl, stir together juices. Add agar-agar and whip together to combine.
4. Pour mixture into a 1-quart (1 L) saucepan over high heat and bring to a boil, about 1–2 minutes. Remove the pan from heat and stir in gelatin until dissolved. Let cool.
5. Pour the liquid into a squeeze bottle with a fine tip.
6. Remove oil from the freezer and drop small droplets of juice into the oil to form the pearls. Let sit about 1 minute, then carefully strain pearls under warm water to rinse excess oil.

TIP: As you drop the liquid into the oil, the droplets will set as they sink slowly.

Homemade Dumplings

These dumplings are so silky and light that you'll barely have to chew. There are two variations that are really fun to make; our popular Flag Dumplings are thin and round, and Spinners resemble little pigtails. Add them to your favorite soups and stews or even dessert sauces for the ultimate comfort food.

Makes 1/2 lb (225 g)

INGREDIENTS
1 1/4 cups (310 mL) all-purpose flour
1 tsp (5 mL) granulated sugar
1/2 tsp (2 mL) salt
1/2 cup (125 mL) water

1. In a medium bowl, combine flour, sugar and salt. Slowly add water while mixing with your hand to form the dough.
2. Dust a clean surface with flour and knead the dough a few times.
3. Pinch off 1-inch (2.5 cm) pieces of dough. Roll each piece back and forth on the surface (dusted with flour) with your hand into pigtails or spinners.

VARIATION: For Flag Dumplings, separate 2-inch (5 cm) pieces of dough, then spread them out with your hands to make thin circular dumplings.
   Set aside on a plate lined with parchment paper. Drop each piece into the soup separately.

EXOTIC CHIPS

Indulge in these delightful treats, flavored with sea salt to enhance the sweetness of the potatoes. Enjoy a tasty guilt-free variation by preparing them in the oven.

Serves 4

1. Preheat a deep fryer with oil to 350°F (180°C).
2. Line a baking sheet with paper towels. Fill a large bowl halfway with cold water and add 1 Tbsp (15 mL) sea salt. Using a mandolin, thinly slice the potatoes. Add to the salted water and soak for 5 minutes to remove some of the excess starch. Dry with paper towels.
3. Place chips in the basket of the deep fryer and fry until crispy, about 3–5 minutes. Transfer to the baking sheet. Salt and serve at once.

VARIATION: Preheat oven to 425°F (220°C). Follow instructions in Step 2, then toss the chips in a bowl with about 1/4 cup (60 mL) vegetable oil. Transfer to the baking sheet lined with parchment and sprinkle with salt. Bake, turning occasionally, until crispy, about 20–25 minutes.

INGREDIENTS

Canola or vegetable oil
Fine sea salt
1 orange-fleshed sweet potato
1 Caribbean sweet potato
1 purple-fleshed potato

HOME-STYLE PEPPERCORN GRAVY

This is a sensational gravy. For years my friends and customers have asked, what's the secret to this tasty gravy? The secret lies beneath.

Makes 1 L

1. In a 4-quart (4 L) pot, heat oil over medium heat. Add flour and cook, stirring, to make a dark brown roux.
2. Stir in drippings. Add stock and bay leaf and bring to a boil. Reduce heat to low.
3. Add thyme, peppercorns and season with salt. Continue to simmer until the gravy is thickened and coats the back of a spoon, about 15 minutes.

TIP: Duck fat is a more-flavorful substitute for vegetable or canola oil.

INGREDIENTS

1/2 cup (125 mL) duck fat or canola oil
2/3 cup (160 mL) all-purpose flour
1/2 cup (125 mL) roast chicken or turkey drippings
4 cups (1 L) chicken stock, heated
1 bay leaf
1/2 tsp (2 mL) ground thyme
1–2 tsp (5–10 mL) tri-color peppercorns
Salt to taste

CITRUS CRANBERRY SAUCE

Why purchase canned cranberry sauce when it only takes 15 minutes of your time to make an exceptional sauce? This citrusy sauce with nuances of ginger is the perfect complement to poultry.
Makes 1L

1. In a 1-quart (1 L) saucepan, combine lemonade and sugar and dissolve over medium heat.
2. Stir in 1 cup (250 mL) of the cranberries. Add zest and ginger and cook until soft, about 5 minutes for frozen cranberries, or 8–10 minutes, if using fresh ones.
3. Add remaining cranberries and salt and continue to cook, stirring, for 5 minutes. Remove from heat and let cool before serving.

TIP: Store in an airtight container in the refrigerator for up to 1 week.

INGREDIENTS

1 cup (250 mL) frozen lemonade concentrate, thawed
1/4 cup (60mL) granulated sugar, optional
1 1/2 cups (375 mL) fresh or frozen cranberries, divided
Zest of 1 orange
2 Tbsp (30 mL) diced candied ginger
1/4 tsp (1 mL) salt

DULCE DE LECHE

1. To prepare the dulce de leche, peel label from can of condensed milk and place can in the center of a 6-quart (6 L) pot. Cover with water by 1 inch (2.5 cm). Place pot over high heat and bring water to a boil. Reduce heat and simmer, about 2 hours.
2. As the water evaporates and top of the can is exposed, add more water to cover. Remove can from pot with tongs and let cool before opening. (This can be prepared a day in advance.)

INGREDIENTS

1 1/4 cups (300 mL) condensed milk

TENDERIZED CONCHS

In The Bahamas, conchs are the "jewel of the sea." They are a labor of love because they have to be tenderized with a mallet before the cooking process. Truly it's worth the effort. If conchs are fresh you may use them in Scotched Conch or Conch Salad recipes and omit the tenderizing process.

Makes 4

INGREDIENTS
4 Queen conches, butterflied
2 tsp (10 mL) baking soda

1. To prepare the conchs, place on a cutting board and, with your hand flat on top, use a sharp knife to slice the meat horizontally at its thickest part, then open it to resemble a butterfly.
2. Place conchs in a large enough pot with water to cover. Add baking soda and simmer over low heat for 2 hours or until conchs are tender.
3. Let conchs cool. Cover with plastic wrap and beat with a mallet on both sides to about 1/4 inch (6 mm) thick.

TIP: It's imperative to bring the conchs to a boil, then reduce the heat to simmer. If the heat is too high the pot will overflow.

VARIATION: Place conchs in a pressure cooker filled two-thirds with water (or follow instructions on the pressure cooker) and cook for about 20 minutes.

CHAPTER 2

BREAKFAST & BRUNCH *In Paradise*

- ELEGANT ISLAND TEA SANDWICHES
- SHEEP TONGUE SOUSE FOR A CROWD
- NASSAU CHICKEN SOUSE
- BOIL FISH & TAITTINGER
- BAHAMIAN OLD-TIME BREAKFAST SANDWICH TWO WAYS
- ELEUTHERA NATIVE FRUIT SALAD
- EXUMA STEW CONCH
- AUNT TIA'S COCONUT JOHNNY CAKE
- CAT ISLAND POTATO BREAD
- NATIVE SKILLET CORNBREAD
- ANDROS NATIVE GRITS
- PANI-CAKES, PANI-CAKES!
- RAGGED ISLAND STEW FISH
- STEAMED HAM WITH GRITS
- CORNED BEEF & EGGS
- STEAMED TUNA WITH GRITS & AVOCADO
- CROOKED ISLAND OATMEAL
- SAIL AWAY ROCK LOBSTER OMELET
- INDEPENDENCE MORNING FRUITY-PUFFED PANCAKE
- SOURSOP PANCAKES WITH HONEY-THYME SYRUP
- SWEET POTATO SPRING FRITTATA
- CRÈME DE BANANA STUFFED FRENCH TOAST

Elegant Island Tea Sandwiches

It's High Tea Time! Impress your guests with these luscious tea sandwiches that will please even the most refined palates.

Corned Beef Salad Sandwiches

Makes 8 sandwiches

1. In a medium bowl, combine corned beef, onion, celery, Scotch bonnet pepper, lime juice and mayonnaise and mix thoroughly with a fork until there are no lumps in the corned beef.
2. Taste and adjust flavor by adding more lime, mayonnaise or pepper, if you prefer spicy.
3. Spread corned beef salad generously over 1 slice of toasted bread, then top with another slice and remove crust.
4. Slice sandwich in half, then half again for miniature tea sandwiches. Set aside on a plate lined with a doily. Repeat with remaining bread and corned beef.

INGREDIENTS

2 cans (each about 3/4 lb/340 g) corned beef
1/2 medium onion, finely diced
1 stalk celery, finely diced
1/2 Scotch bonnet pepper, finely diced
Juice of 2 limes
1/2 cup (125 mL) mayonnaise
1/2 loaf sliced white bread, lightly toasted

Spicy Tuna Salad Sandwiches

Makes 8 sandwiches

1. Using a mandolin with the guard, carefully slice cucumbers thinly and set aside.
2. In a medium bowl, combine tuna, onion, celery, Scotch bonnet pepper, lime juice and mayonnaise and mix thoroughly.
3. Season with salt to taste and garnish with paprika.
4. Spread Mustard and Chili Lime mayonnaise on slices of bread and place 2 slices of cucumber on top of each. Generously spread tuna salad over cucumbers and top with the other slices of bread.
5. Remove crusts. Repeat with other slices and place on a plate lined with a doily.

INGREDIENTS

2 English cucumbers, thinly sliced
4 cans (each 6 oz/170 g) tuna, drained (about 4 cups/1 L)
1/2 medium onion, finely diced
1 stalk celery, finely diced
1 Scotch bonnet pepper, finely diced
Juice of 3 limes
1 1/2 cups (375 mL) mayonnaise
1/2 tsp (2 mL) salt
1/4 tsp (1 mL) smoked paprika
1/2 loaf sliced whole wheat or rye bread, lightly toasted
1 cup (250 mL) Mustard & Chili Lime Mayonnaise (see recipe, page 12)

Curry Chicken Salad Sandwiches
Makes 8 sandwiches

1. In a skillet, heat oil over medium heat. Add curry powder and cumin and cook, stirring to release the oils, for 3 minutes. Add cream and continue cooking for another 2 minutes. Remove from heat and set aside.
2. In a large bowl, combine shredded chicken, vinegar, onion, celery, bell pepper, Scotch bonnet pepper (if using), mayonnaise, mustard and lemon juice and mix.
3. Add curry sauce to the chicken and mix well. Fold in raisins and season with salt and black pepper to taste. Spread salad generously on 1 slice toasted bread. Top with lettuce and carrots and cover with another slice of bread. Remove crust and cut into 4 pieces. Repeat with other bread slices. Add to the plates with the other tea sandwiches for a variety.

INGREDIENTS

3 Tbsp (45 mL) vegetable oil
2 Tbsp (30 mL) Caribbean curry powder
1/4 tsp (1 mL) ground cumin
1 cup (250 mL) coconut cream
6 cooked chicken thighs, shredded
1 Tbsp (15 mL) red wine vinegar
1/2 medium onion, diced
1 stalk celery, diced
1/2 red bell pepper, diced
1/2 Scotch bonnet pepper, finely diced (optional)
1 cup (250 mL) mayonnaise
1/2 tsp (2 mL) Dijon mustard
Juice of 1 lemon
2 Tbsp (30 mL) sultanas (golden raisins)
Salt and pepper to taste
1/2 loaf sliced multi-grain bread, lightly toasted
3 slices romaine lettuce, leaves shredded
3 rainbow carrots, julienned

SHEEP TONGUE SOUSE FOR A CROWD

Sheep tongue souse is a lime and chili–based soup that is unique to The Bahamas. There are no thickening agents added as this souse receives its silky aspic texture from the protein (similar to a consommé). Tongue may not appeal to everyone but once you've tasted this delicious souse, it will have you craving for more. If tongue meat doesn't entice you substitute with mutton.

Serves 6

1. Fill a 6-quart (6 L) pot halfway with water and place over medium heat. Add 1/4 cup (60 mL) vinegar and bring to a boil.
2. Add sheep's tongue pieces and par-cook, about 10 minutes. Drain in a colander.
3. Fill pot halfway with water again, return meat to pot and bring to a boil. Add onion, celery, bay leaf, thyme and allspice berries. Cover pot with a lid slightly ajar (allowing steam to escape), then reduce heat to simmer and cook for 30 minutes.
4. Add remaining vinegar, lime juice, allspice, thyme, salt and pepper sauce. Reduce heat and simmer for 15 minutes more.
5. Ladle the souse into bowls, and garnish with celery leaves.

> **TIPS:** Serve with lime wedges, potato bread or slices of Aunt Tia's Coconut Johnny Cake sliced (see recipe, page 34).
>
> If unprocessed sheep's tongue is your only option at the supermarket, then process (removing the outer layer) by adding 1/4 cup (60 mL) of white vinegar. Bring to a boil, then reduce and simmer for about 30 minutes. Let cool, then slide the outer layer off and discard; continue to process by dicing the meat into 1/2-inch (1 cm) pieces, then follow steps 1 through 5.
>
> In North America, you may purchase sheep tongue packages (cleaned and diced) at most Asian supermarkets or specialty meat stores.

INGREDIENTS

5 Tbsp (75 mL) white vinegar, divided
3 lbs (1.4 kg) sheep's tongue, diced
1 medium onion, sliced
2 stalks celery, diced
1 bay leaf
1 tsp (5 mL) dried thyme leaves
1 Tbsp (15 mL) allspice berries
Juice of 4 limes
1/2 tsp (2 mL) ground allspice
1/2 tsp (2 mL) ground thyme
Fine sea salt to taste
1/4 cup (60 mL) Bahamian Pepper Sauce or to taste (see recipe, page 3)
1 Tbsp (15 mL) celery leaves, chiffonade, for garnish

Nassau Chicken Souse

Chicken souse is the Bahamian version of chicken soup. It's an authentic "feel-good" type of soup. Whenever Bahamians are feeling "under the weather," we venture to our local souse house restaurant for this medicinal piquant and tangy souse. Try it over native yellow grits . . . delish!
Serves 6

1. In an 8-quart (8 L) pot, place chicken with enough water to cover over high heat. Add vinegar, 1 Tbsp (15 mL) crushed allspice berries and bay leaf. Bring to a boil and cook for 10 minutes.
2. Remove pot from heat, pour into a colander and discard water, reserving chicken.
3. Return empty pot to medium heat. Add onion, celery, whole allspice berries, thyme and lime juice. Place chicken over vegetables, cover tightly with a lid and let sweat for 15 minutes (this is the base for a flavorful souse).
4. Add enough water to cover by 3 inches (8 cm), stir and bring to a boil with lid slightly ajar to release steam.
5. Add remaining lime juice, salt and pepper sauce, stir and continue cooking, about 15–20 minutes more until chicken is no longer pink inside. Adjust seasoning, adding more salt to taste, ladle into bowls and garnish with celery leaves.

TIP: Serve with a side of grits or buttery Aunt Tia's Coconut Johnny Cake (see recipe, page 34).

INGREDIENTS

5-lb (2.2 kg) bag chicken wings including drumettes (separated)
1/4 cup (60 mL) white vinegar
1 Tbsp (15 mL) allspice berries, crushed
1 bay leaf
1 medium onion, sliced and cut in half
2 stalks celery, diced
1 Tbsp (15 mL) whole allspice berries
1 tsp (5 mL) fresh thyme leaves
Juice of 8 limes, divided
2 Tbsp (30 mL) sea salt
1/4 cup (60 mL) Bahamian Pepper Sauce (see recipe, page 3)
1 Tbsp (15 mL) celery leaves

BOIL FISH & TAITTINGER

"Raquel, it's an emergency," said our friend Dennis Ledard. "Tell your husband I just caught a grouper that's so fresh it's still moving; I'm about to make Boil Fish and I put the Taittinger on ice so drop everything… let's have a food orgy!" I've never met another chef in the food industry as charismatic and passionate about food as Dennis Ledard, "who lived to eat well." Thanks for the memories. Enjoy this dish with a crisp cold glass of Taittinger champagne.

Serves 4

1. Rinse grouper and pat dry with paper towels. Place on a baking sheet or large plate lined with parchment paper. Squeeze juice of 2 limes over fish, then rub both sides with fish seasoning.
2. In a wide-bottomed 4-quart (4 L) pot, add oil over low heat. Add salted pork and render for 3 minutes until golden.
3. Reduce heat to low, add onion, celery and potatoes. Position fish on top of vegetables and cover tightly with a lid. Let vegetables sweat and simmer, about 15–20 minutes for a flavorful stock.
4. Add enough water to cover fish by 1/2 inch (1 cm). Increase heat to medium-low. Add thyme and cook until potatoes are tender when pierced with a knife, about 30 minutes.
5. Add remaining lime juice and adjust salt, if necessary. Let simmer for another 5 minutes making sure not to overcook the delicate fish.
6. Add pepper sauce (if using) and gently stir.

TIPS: Serve immediately with a side of buttery yellow grits or Aunt Tia's Coconut Johnny Cake (see recipe, page 34) slices and enjoy.

Ask your local fishmonger to scale and chop the fish into 2-inch (5 cm) pieces (bone-in preferably).

INGREDIENTS

2 1/2 lbs (1.1 kg) grouper, roughly chopped
Juice of 4 limes, divided
2 Tbsp (30 mL) Bahama Fish Seasoning (see recipe, page 2)
1 Tbsp (15 mL) vegetable oil
2 oz (60 g) salted pork, diced
1/2 medium onion, sliced and cut in half
1 stalk celery, diced
1 russet potato, diced
1 tsp (5 mL) fresh thyme leaves
Fine sea salt to taste
2 Tbsp (30 mL) Bahamian Pepper Sauce (see recipe, page 3) (optional)

Bahamian Old Time Breakfast Sandwich Two Ways

It's not a traditional Bahamian breakfast sandwich without an over-easy egg that explodes with the first bite and drips onto the plate mixing with all the necessary condiments to make it juicy!
Serves 4

Johnny Cake Open Face Sandwiches

1. To make guava butter, add the paste to a small microwave-safe bowl with 1 tsp (5 mL) water. Soften guava paste in the microwave for 2 minutes. Mix then fold paste into softened butter and set aside.
2. Preheat oven to broil on high. Place bacon over a rack and place on top of a baking sheet. Let cook until crispy, flipping over after 4 minutes, about 8 minutes. Set aside.
3. Lightly toast johnny cake slices in the oven and set aside on a platter.
4. In a large skillet, melt 2 Tbsp (30 mL) butter with 1 Tbsp (15 mL) oil over medium-low heat. Break eggs into pan, keeping the delicate yolk intact. Season with salt and pepper. Then flip eggs gently and cook to over easy.
5. Spread guava butter generously over one side of each slice then return to the plate with the butter side facing up.
6. Warm cheese in a skillet and place on top of butter with a spatula. Top with lettuce, 2 slices of tomatoes, 2 strips bacon, then egg.
7. Garnish with Sriracha and parsley, repeat with other slices.

INGREDIENTS
Guava Butter
1 Tbsp (15 mL) guava paste
1/2 cup (125 mL) butter, softened

8 slices bacon
4 slices Aunt Tia's Coconut Johnny Cake, cut 1 1/2 inches (4 cm) thick (see recipe, page 34)
3 Tbsp (45 mL) butter
1 Tbsp (15 mL) olive oil
4 large eggs
Salt and pepper to taste
4 green leaf or butter lettuce
8 slices colorful heirloom or beefsteak tomatoes, divided
4 slices cheddar cheese
1 Tbsp (15 mL) hot sauce or Sriracha (optional)
2 tsp (10 mL) diced fresh Italian parsley

Cinnamon Raisin Sandwiches

1. Toast bread slices and generously spread mayonnaise on one side of each slice of bread.
2. In a large skillet, melt 3 Tbsp (45 mL) oil over medium heat and fry bologna until a little crispy on both sides.
3. Layer cinnamon raisin bread with lettuce, 2 slices of tomatoes, bologna, cheese then top with egg, top with the other slice of bread, and enjoy with lemongrass tea or refreshing Mimosas!

INGREDIENTS

8 thick slices cinnamon raisin bread, toasted

1 cup (250 mL) Mustard & Chili Lime Mayonnaise (see recipe, page 12)

3 Tbsp (45 mL) olive oil

4 large eggs

4 slices cheddar cheese

4 slices bologna sausage or honey-glazed ham

4 leaves green or butter lettuce

8 slices colorful heirloom or beefsteak tomatoes, divided

Parliament Square, Nassau, Bahamas

ELEUTHERA NATIVE FRUIT SALAD

The Island of Eleuthera is known for its mesmerizing Pink Sand Beach on Harbour Island, where the sand is literally pink from the speckles of corals and shells that are washed ashore. It's also known worldwide for having the most naturally sweet pineapples. It is believed that The Bahamas was the first country to produce pineapples on a commercial scale. In the late 1880s, pineapples were its major export with over 90,000 dozen shipped to the United States and England.

Serves 6

1. Place all ingredients in a large bowl and mix well. Serve chilled in hollow pineapples or coconut shells and enjoy a taste of paradise.

   TIP: Kent, Kensington or Ataulfo mangoes are readily available in supermarkets. The flesh is a deep golden yellow that is smooth, creamy and not fibrous like other mangoes, making them appropriate for this recipe.

INGREDIENTS

3 cups (750 mL) diced pineapples
2 ripe Kent or Kensington mangoes, diced
2 gala apples, diced
1 cup (250 mL) honeydew melon
1 cup (250 mL) cantaloupe
1 cup (250 mL) pitted cherries, drained
1/4 cup (60 mL) confectioner's (icing) sugar
Juice of 1 lemon
2 cups (500 mL) coconut water with pieces of jelly
2 cups (500 mL) pineapple juice
2 cups (500 mL) mango juice
2 Tbsp (30 mL) spiced rum (optional)
6 hollow pineapples or coconut shells for serving (optional)

Exuma Stew Conch

This ambrosial stew is made with morsels of tender conch meat. Throughout North America, Queen conchs are readily available for purchase at Asian supermarkets or seafood distributors.
Serves 6

1. Follow the instructions to tenderize the conch meat (see recipe, page 18) and reserve the flavorful stock. Dice meat into bite-size pieces and set aside.
2. In a separate 8-quart (8 L) pot, heat oil over medium heat and cook flour while stirring to make a dark brown roux.
3. Add onions, potatoes and carrots and cook, stirring occasionally, for 3 minutes.
4. Add paste, tomatoes and thyme leaves and cook for 2 minutes more.
5. Pour in 8 cups (2 L) reserved stock while stirring (be cautious of the steam), for a smooth roux that coats the back of the spoon.
6. Add bay leaf and conch meat and bring to a boil. Reduce heat and simmer to cook for 30 minutes.
7. Add lime juice and season with salt and pepper. Add 1–2 Tbsp (15–30 mL) pepper sauce (if using) and simmer for 5 minutes more. Serve at once with slices of yummy potato bread.

TIP: Caribbean sweet potatoes are also known as boniatos. They are a sweet potato with dry white flesh, pink-purplish skin and a gentle sweet chestnut flavor.

INGREDIENTS

5 lbs (2.2 kg) Queen conchs
1/2 cup (125 mL) vegetable oil
2/3 cup (160 mL) all-purpose flour
1/2 medium onion, sliced
2 Caribbean sweet potatoes, diced (see page 223)
1 large carrot, diced
1 tsp (5 mL) tomato paste
1 ripe tomato, diced
2 tsp (10 mL) fresh thyme leaves
1 bay leaf
Juice of 1 lime
Salt and pepper to taste
2 Tbsp (30 mL) Bahamian Pepper Sauce (see recipe, page 3) (optional)

AUNT TIA'S COCONUT JOHNNY CAKE

The origins of johnny cake dates back to the 18th century. Fishermen and sailors made this bread on the decks of their vessels by building a fire in a box that was filled with sand to keep the flames from spreading to the craft. It was originally called journey cake because it was quick to make and sustainable while travelling. Taste a piece of history with my aunt's legendary recipe.

Serves 8

1. Preheat oven to 350°F (180°C). Grease an 8-inch (20 cm) square baking dish with butter.
2. In a large bowl, combine flour, baking powder, sugar and salt and mix together.
3. Add butter and, using your hand, combine with flour by breaking up into smaller pieces. Add coconut, oil and mix.
4. Slowly pour in milk while mixing with your other hand to form dough into a ball (the dough should be soft and easy to handle). Dust a clean surface with flour and knead dough a few times.
5. Place dough in the baking dish, spread out and level with your hands. Pour cream over and bake, about 45 minutes until the top is golden or a toothpick inserted into the center comes out clean. Serve warm with guava or mango jam.

VARIATION: For Aunt Tia's Johnny Cake, follow the recipe above but omit the coconut.

INGREDIENTS

2 cups (500 mL) all-purpose flour
2 Tbsp (30 mL) baking powder
1 cup (250 mL) granulated sugar
1/4 tsp (1 mL) salt
1/4 cup (60 mL) butter, cubed
1/2 cup (125 mL) frozen grated coconut, thawed
2 Tbsp (30 mL) canola or vegetable oil
1 cup (250 mL) whole milk
1/4 cup (60 mL) whipping (or heavy) cream (35%)

CAT ISLAND POTATO BREAD

This is a perfect accompaniment to any stew or soup in The Bahamas. Sweet Caribbean potatoes are combined with flour and spices to form a bread that is divine. I've had many variations of this alluring, tasty spiced bread, but Mrs. Turner's Cat Island recipe is simply the best! Whenever I make this potato bread, I reflect on her attention to detail while baking in her tranquil kitchen, infused with captivating aromas.

Serves 12

1. Preheat oven to 350°F (180°C). Grease a 13- x 9-inch (33 x 23 cm) baking pan with 3 Tbsp (45 mL) of the lard. Sprinkle with a little flour and shake off any excess flour.
2. Peel potatoes and place in a medium bowl with cold water, then grate potatoes on the fine side of a grater or in the bowl of a food processor with the fine-shredding side of the wheel attachment. Transfer potatoes to a large bowl.
3. Add grated coconut, sugar, salt and 1/2 cup (125 mL) water and mix well with your hands. Add flour and remaining lard and continue mixing thoroughly.
4. Add black pepper, cinnamon and another 1/2 cup (125 mL) water (the consistency should feel like a pudding, add more water, if needed).
5. Transfer mixture to the baking pan and bake in the center of the oven for 2 hours (cover loosely with foil after 1 hour to maintain the color). Let cool to a warm temperature and enjoy.

INGREDIENTS

1/2 cup (125 mL) lard, cubed, divided
2 large Caribbean sweet potatoes (reddish skin)
1/2 cup (125 mL) frozen grated coconut, thawed
3 cups (750 mL) granulated sugar
1 tsp (5 mL) salt
1 cup (250 mL) water, divided
2 1/2 cups (625 mL) all-purpose flour
1/2 tsp (2 mL) freshly ground black pepper
1 tsp (5 mL) ground cinnamon

NATIVE SKILLET CORNBREAD

During the 18th century, johnny cakes were prepared with corn or maize and called ash or hoe cakes because they were cooked on a garden tool over fire. There are debates whether the recipe was brought to The Bahamas by British colonists or if it originated with the native Indians. I'm thankful that this unique bread is a part of my heritage. I've enjoyed it over the years as an accompaniment to barbecues, soups and stews. Sour cream and coconut milk make this the most luscious and decadent native cornbread.

Serves 8

1. Preheat oven to 350°F (180°C).
2. In a large bowl, combine flour, cornmeal, sugar, baking powder, baking soda and salt and form a well in the center.
3. In a small bowl, whisk together sour cream, coconut milk and bacon drippings. Pour 2 cups (500 mL) of this mixture into the center of the flour mixture and mix well to combine.
4. Fold in bacon, corn, coconut and Scotch bonnet pepper (if using).
5. In a 10-inch (25 cm) cast-iron ovenproof skillet, melt butter over low heat. Pour batter into the skillet and level with a spatula. Pour remaining milk mixture over batter and bake, about 30–35 minutes or until the center is firm to the touch.
6. Let cool for 5 minutes and serve warm.

INGREDIENTS

1 cup (250 mL) all-purpose flour
1 cup (250 mL) yellow cornmeal
1 cup (250 mL) granulated sugar
2 tsp (10 mL) baking powder
1/2 tsp (2 mL) baking soda
1/2 tsp (2 mL) salt
1/2 cup (125 mL) sour cream
2 1/4 cups (560 mL) coconut milk
4 strips bacon, cooked and crumbled (reserving drippings)
1 cup (250 mL) fresh or frozen corn kernels, thawed
1/2 cup (125 mL) frozen grated coconut, thawed
1/4 green Scotch bonnet pepper, diced (seeds removed and discarded) (optional)
2 Tbsp (30 mL) butter

ANDROS NATIVE GRITS

The island of Andros is known for producing some of the best cooks in The Bahamas, and my grandmother happens to be one of them. The cuisine is comforting and unpretentious. Hominy (or yellow grits) is the staple breakfast comfort food eaten by itself as a porridge or as an accompaniment to eggs, corn beef, souses and stews. The older generation prefers to add a slice of avocado.

Serves 4

1. Fill a 3-quart (3 L) pot over high heat with water. Add oil and salt and bring to a boil.
2. Reduce heat to low and remove the pot. Stir in grits (to avoid lumps), then return pot to low heat. Cover with a lid slightly ajar and cook, about 5 minutes.
3. Add butter and stir. Adjust seasoning. You may add your favorite combination of cheeses to make cheese grits, if preferred. Serve at once.

INGREDIENTS

4 cups (1 L) water
2 Tbsp (30 mL) olive oil
1 tsp (5 mL) salt
1 cup (250 mL) fine or coarse
   yellow grits
1/4 cup (60 mL) butter, cubed

Pani-Cakes, Pani-Cakes!

These marvelous treats are the Bahamian version of pancakes.
They're fried delights, no maple syrup is needed. I challenge you
to try and eat just one.
Serves 4

1. Preheat a deep fryer with oil to 325°F (160°C).
2. In a large bowl, combine flour, baking powder, sugar and salt
   and mix. Slowly pour in water while whisking the batter to a
   smooth consistency.
3. Add mashed bananas and fold into batter. Using a stainless-
   steel spoon, scoop up and drop batter into the hot oil and fry
   for 3 minutes on each side until golden and done.
4. Line a plate with paper towels and place pani-cakes on top,
   sprinkle with confectioner's sugar and keep warm in the
   oven until ready to serve.

INGREDIENTS

Canola or vegetable oil
2 cups (500 mL) all-purpose flour
1 Tbsp (30 mL) baking powder
1 cup (250 mL) granulated sugar
1/2 tsp (2 mL) salt
1 cup (250 mL) water
1 ripe banana, mashed
1/4 cup (60 mL) confectioner's
   (icing) sugar

RAGGED ISLAND STEW FISH

A food blogger once said, "Bahamians don't make a big deal about breakfast." Contrary to fact, breakfast is one of the most important meals to us. In our culture, it's savored and celebrated on the weekends while spending quality time with our families and friends. There are many restaurants and souse shacks, whose businesses survive solely by catering to the breakfast crowd. Many might find it odd that we eat seafood for breakfast, but "when in Rome!"

Serves 4

1. Rinse fish in salted water and pat dry with paper towels. Squeeze lime juice over fish and season on both sides with the seasoning.
2. In a large skillet, add 1/2 cup (125 mL) of the oil over medium heat. Fry fish until skin is brown and crispy on both sides, but not cooked all the way through, about 3 minutes per side. Set aside on a plate lined with paper towels.
3. In an 8-quart (8 L) pot, add remaining vegetable oil over medium heat. Add flour and stir to make a dark brown roux.
4. Add onion and cook for 2 minutes. Add paste, tomato and thyme and cook, stirring, for 2 minutes more.
5. Pour in stock, stirring, and then bring to a boil. Add fish. Reduce heat to low and simmer for 20 minutes.
6. Add lime juice, salt, pepper and pepper sauce and continue cooking for 5 minutes more.

TIP: Serve over yellow grits, add a slice of potato bread and don't forget the Eleuthera fruit salad!

INGREDIENTS

2 1/2 lbs (1.1 kg) grouper, cut into 2-inch (5 cm) strips
Juice of 3 limes, divided
Salt
1/4 cup (60 mL) Bahama Fish Seasoning (see recipe, page 2)
1 cup (250 mL) vegetable oil, divided
2/3 cup (160 mL) all-purpose flour
1/2 medium onion, sliced
1 tsp (5 mL) tomato paste
1 ripe tomato, diced
2 tsp (10 mL) fresh thyme leaves
8 cups (2 L) fish stock or water, heated
2 Tbsp (30 mL) Bahamian Pepper Sauce (see recipe, page 3)
Salt and pepper to taste

STEAMED HAM WITH GRITS

This is our family's traditional Christmas and New Year's breakfast. Don't wait for the holidays to indulge. After all, any morning spent eating together is a special day. My aunt Tia was responsible for making the most succulent leg of smoked ham with a whisky and brown sugar glaze for the holidays, and she always made sure to set aside enough ham for the morning after. Whenever I'm craving that luscious meal, I simply purchase a precooked honey-glazed ham from the supermarket.

Serves 4

1. In a large skillet, heat oil over medium heat. Add onions and sweat until translucent, about 3 minutes. Add pepper and garlic and cook until fragrant, about 1 minute.
2. Add tomatoes and continue to cook for 3 minutes.
3. Add ketchup, molasses and water and bring to a boil, then reduce and simmer for 5 minutes to make a gravy that coats the back of a spoon.
4. Stir in thyme and ham. Add cloves, parsley and season with salt and pepper to taste. Continue to simmer for 10 minutes and serve over creamy grits.

INGREDIENTS

3 Tbsp (45 mL) olive oil
1/2 medium sweet white onion, sliced
1/2 green bell pepper, diced
4 cloves garlic, finely diced
1 cup (250 mL) tomatoes, diced
1/4 cup (60 mL) ketchup
1 Tbsp (15 mL) molasses
1/2 cup (125 mL) water
1 tsp (5 mL) fresh thyme leaves
6 cups (1.5 L) prepared honey-glazed ham, cut into 1-inch (2.5 cm) pieces
1 tsp (5 mL) ground cloves
1 Tbsp (15 mL) chopped fresh Italian parsley
Salt and pepper to taste
Andros Native Grits (see recipe, page 37)

CORNED BEEF & EGGS

This old-time favorite dates back to the 1700s. It was introduced to The Bahamas by British Loyalists.

Serves 6

1. In a large skillet, heat oil over medium heat. Add potato and cook, stirring, for 3 minutes.
2. Add onion and bell pepper and cook for 3 minutes.
3. Add thyme and tomatoes with juice and cook for 3 minutes more. Add corned beef. Separate pieces with a cooking spoon, stirring to break up any lumps.
4. Stir in ketchup, Worcestershire and hot sauce (if using). Let simmer for 10 minutes.
5. Meanwhile, in another large skillet over medium heat, add butter and cook eggs to over easy. Keep warm.
6. Serve corned beef topped with 2 over-easy eggs. Garnish with hot sauce and parsley for a tasty presentation.

INGREDIENTS

2 Tbsp (30 mL) olive oil

1 russet potato, diced

1/2 medium onion, sliced

1/4 piece green bell pepper, diced

1/2 tsp (2 mL) fresh thyme leaves

1/2 cup (125 mL) fire-roasted diced tomatoes with sauce

2 cans (each about 3/4 lb/340 g) corned beef

3 Tbsp (45 mL) ketchup

1 Tbsp (15 mL) Worcestershire sauce

2 tsp (10 mL) hot pepper sauce (optional)

3 Tbsp (45 mL) butter

8 large eggs

Parsley, for garnish

Steamed Tuna with Grits & Avocado

Fresh seafood is always best but there are times when canned tuna will do, as in this tasty dish.

Serves 4

1. In a large skillet, heat oil over medium heat. Add onion, garlic and green and red bell peppers and cook for 3 minutes.
2. Add thyme and tomatoes with sauce and simmer for 3 minutes more.
3. Stir in tuna and cook for 5 minutes. Add juice of 1 lime, ketchup, pepper sauce, salt and pepper. Reduce heat to low and simmer for 5 minutes.
4. Meanwhile, squeeze juice of 1/2 lime over avocado slices and drizzle with honey. Serve tuna over white or yellow grits with a slice of avocado.

INGREDIENTS

3 Tbsp (45 mL) olive oil

1/2 medium onion, diced

2 cloves garlic, diced

1/4 cup (60 mL) diced green bell pepper

1/4 cup (60 mL) diced red bell pepper

1 tsp (5 mL) dried thyme leaves

1/2 cup (125 mL) fire-roasted tomatoes with sauce

4 cans (each 6 oz/170 g) tuna, drained (about 4 cups/1 L)

Juice of 1 1/2 limes, divided

3 Tbsp (45 mL) ketchup

2 tsp (10 mL) Caribbean pepper sauce

Salt and pepper to taste

1 ripe avocado, cut into 4 slices

2 Tbsp (30 mL) honey

Andros Native Grits (see recipe, page 37)

CROOKED ISLAND OATMEAL

Here's a taste of paradise in a bowl, the ultimate comfort food on a rainy day.

Serves 2

1. In a saucepan, heat milk over medium heat. When tiny bubbles start to form stir in oats. Let simmer for 5 minutes.
2. Stir in condensed milk. Add cinnamon, nutmeg, vanilla and almond extract and cook for 3 minutes.
3. Fold in coconut and guava. Remove from heat and ladle into bowls.
4. Top with 3 mango slices and garnish with toasted almonds. Serve at once.

INGREDIENTS

3 cups (750 mL) whole milk or almond milk
1 1/2 cups (375 mL) steel-cut oats
1/2 cup (125 mL) condensed milk or 2 Tbsp (30 mL) granulated sugar
1 tsp (5 mL) ground cinnamon
1 tsp (5 mL) fresh grated nutmeg
1 tsp (5 mL) pure vanilla extract
1 tsp (5 mL) almond extract
1/4 cup (60 mL) sweetened coconut, shredded
1/4 cup (60 mL) diced guavas

Garnish

Mango or mamey slices, for garnish
1 Tbsp (15 mL) toasted sliced almonds, for garnish

Sail Away Rock Lobster Omelet

The Bahamas is known for the spiny tail or rock lobster that inhabits our warm waters. They do not have claws like cold water lobsters but they're just as delicate and tasty. Enjoy a breakfast fit for a king or queen.

Serves 4

1. In a medium bowl, whisk eggs while pouring in cream. Season with salt and pepper and set aside.
2. To prepare the gremolata, in a small bowl, combine diced tomatoes, garlic, parsley, lemon zest and juice. Set aside.
3. To prepare the avocado crème, remove the flesh of the avocado and place in the bowl of a food processor. Add lemon juice and purée. Transfer to a small bowl and fold in sour cream. Season to taste, cover with plastic wrap and refrigerate
4. To prepare the lobster filling, season lobster with seafood seasoning. In a medium skillet over medium heat, cook lobster until opaque, about 1–2 minutes. Transfer to a small bowl.
5. Return skillet to medium heat and add oil. Cook onions and red and green bell peppers for 3 minutes.
6. Add corn kernels, green onions, parsley, ground fennel and cayenne. Adjust seasoning and cook for 2 minutes more.
7. Remove from heat. Transfer to a bowl and fold in goat and cream cheeses and set aside.
8. Return skillet to low heat and add butter and half of the egg mixture to make an omelet. When omelet is partially cooked and set in the center, add half of the corn filling and gently spread out with a spatula.
9. Place half of the lobster over the corn mixture, then fold omelet over to seal. Transfer to a plate and keep warm, repeating with the other omelet.
10. To serve, cut the omelets in half on the diagonal, top with the Gremolata and Avocado Crème.

INGREDIENTS

1 dozen large eggs
2 Tbsp (30 mL) half-and-half cream (10%)
1/4 tsp (2 mL) salt
1/4 tsp (2 mL) freshly ground black pepper

Gremolata
1 cup (250 mL) diced ripe tomatoes
4 cloves garlic, roasted and diced
1/2 tsp (2 mL) diced fresh Italian parsley
Zest and juice of 1/2 lemon

Avocado Crème
1 ripe avocado
1 tsp (5 mL) lemon juice
2 cups (500 mL) sour cream

Lobster Filling
1 lb (450 g) lobster meat (about 2 cups/500 mL)
2 tsp (10 mL) seafood seasoning
3 Tbsp (45 mL) olive oil
1/2 red onion, diced
1/4 red bell pepper, finely diced
1/4 orange bell pepper, finely diced
2 ears peaches and cream corn, cooked and kernels removed
1/2 cup (125 mL) diced green onions
1 tsp (5 mL) diced fresh Italian parsley

continued on next page

1 Tbsp (15 mL) fennel seeds,
  roasted and ground
Pinch of cayenne pepper
Salt and pepper to taste
1 cup (250 mL) goat cheese, crumbled
1/2 cup (125 mL) cream cheese,
  softened
1/4 cup (60 mL) butter

INDEPENDENCE MORNING FRUITY PUFFED PANCAKE

The Bahamas achieved full independence from Britain on July 10th, 1973. Celebrate your country's anniversary by decorating this delightful puffed pancake in the fashion of your country's flag and take a photo because it won't last long.

Serves 6

1. To prepare the pancake batter, preheat oven to 400°F (200°C). Add butter to a 13- x 9-inch (33 x 23 cm) baking pan and place in the oven to melt.
2. Combine remaining batter ingredients in a large bowl and mix well.
3. Remove pan from the oven and pour 1/4 cup (60 mL) of the butter into pancake mixture and continue to whisk. Pour pancake batter into the hot baking pan and return to the oven. Bake for 40 minutes until golden and center sets. (The pancake will deflate slightly after it's removed from the oven.)
4. To prepare the mango filling, in a saucepan over medium heat, pour in rice wine and simmer. Add mangoes and cook until slightly softened. Add lemon juice and ground cinnamon and stir. Cook until liquid is reduced by half. Remove from heat and set aside.
5. To prepare the cornstarch mixture, mix cornstarch in cold water and set aside.
6. Cook blackberries and blueberries separately by placing 1-quart (1 L) saucepans over medium heat. Divide cornstarch the mixture and stir into the berries.
7. Add all remaining ingredients to individual blackberry and blueberry fillings while stirring until sugar dissolves and mixture is slightly thickened. Remove from heat.
8. To assemble, use skewers to separate the layers of fruits while designing your country's flag. Spoon the fruits within the lines, then remove the skewers and display as a centerpiece on the table.

TIP: Use fruits or berries that are the same colors of your country's flag.

INGREDIENTS

Pancake Batter
1/2 cup (125 mL) butter
1 cup (250 mL) all-purpose flour
1/4 tsp (1 mL) ground cinnamon
1 Tbsp (15 mL) granulated sugar
2 cups (500 mL) whole milk
3 eggs
1/2 tsp (2 mL) salt

Mango Filling
1/2 cup (125 mL) rice wine (mirin)
2 cups (500 mL) fresh or frozen
  mango chunks
Juice of 1/2 lemon
1/4 tsp (1 mL) ground cinnamon

Cornstarch Mixture
4 tsp (20 mL) cornstarch
2 Tbsp (30 mL) cold water

Blackberry Filling
2 cups (500 mL) fresh blackberries
1/2 cup (125 mL) granulated sugar or
  1/4 cup (60 mL) honey
Pinch of salt
1/2 tsp (2 mL) ground cinnamon

Blueberry Filling
2 cups (500 mL) fresh blueberries
1/2 cup (125 mL) granulated sugar or
  1/4 cup (60 mL) honey
1/4 tsp (1 mL) salt
1/4 tsp (1 mL) ground cinnamon
1/4 tsp (1 mL) ground nutmeg

Soursop Pancakes with Honey-Thyme Syrup

I grew up eating this unique heart-shaped, prickly yellowish green fruit in fruit cups, blended drinks and ice cream. Soursop ranges in size from 4–12 inches (10–30 cm) long and up to 6 inches (15 cm) in width and weighs up to 10–15 lbs (4.5–6.8 kg). Its inner surface is cream-colored, fibrous, soft and juicy with hard black seeds that are 1/2–3/4 inches (1.25 to 2 cm) long. Soursop (also known as custard apple or guanabana) has a unique acidic yet mellow-honeyed flavor profile. As a fruit that is native to the Caribbean, it's certainly "the cream of the crop."

Serves 4

1. To prepare honey-thyme syrup, in a small saucepan, combine water, honey, thyme and ginger over medium heat and stir until honey dissolves.
2. Bring to a boil, then reduce heat to simmer, stirring occasionally, for 5 minutes. Reduce heat and keep warm.
3. To prepare soursop pancakes, in a large bowl, combine dry ingredients and make a well in the center.
4. Pour milk in the center while mixing thoroughly to make the batter. Fold in soursop pulp.
5. In a griddle or skillet, melt 1 Tbsp (15 mL) butter over medium-low heat. Pour 1/2 cup (125 mL) of the batter in the pan and cook on 1 side until tiny bubbles form on top. Flip pancake over to cook on other side until golden.
6. Keep warm in the oven. Serve drizzled with the syrup and topped with whipped cream.

INGREDIENTS

Honey-Thyme Syrup
1/2 cup (125 mL) water
1/2 cup (125 mL) honey
3 sprigs fresh thyme
1/2 tsp (2 mL) grated fresh ginger

Soursop Pancakes
1 1/2 cups (375 mL) all-purpose flour
1/2 tsp (2 mL) ground ginger
1/4 tsp (1 mL) ground nutmeg
1 Tbsp (15 mL) baking powder
1/2 cup (125 mL) granulated sugar
1/4 tsp (1 mL) salt
2 cups (500 mL) whole milk
1 cup (250 mL) frozen soursop pulp, thawed
1/2 cup (125 mL) butter, divided
2 cups (500 mL) whipped cream, for garnish

Sweet Potato Spring Frittata

My friend Jai is a talented pianist and singer who happens to make the best frittatas. She uses shredded potatoes as the base of her frittatas, that way the potato is crispy and the egg mixture is cooked to perfection. Enjoy an island twist to this tasty dish with a sweet potato crispy crust. It's perfect for a weekend brunch!

Serves 4

1. Preheat oven to broil on high.
2. In a large cast-iron ovenproof skillet, heat 3 Tbsp (45 mL) of the oil over medium heat. Add pancetta and cook until crispy. Set aside in a small bowl.
3. Add red and orange peppers, broccoli and cauliflower to skillet and cook for 3 minutes. Set aside.
4. Season grated sweet potatoes with salt and pepper. Add to skillet and drizzle with remaining oil and pack down in the skillet with a spatula to cover the bottom of the pan. Place skillet in oven and broil on high, about 3–5 minutes.
5. Meanwhile, break eggs into a bowl and whisk in cream. Season with salt and pepper. Using oven-proofed gloves, remove skillet from the oven and pour eggs over the potatoes.
6. Place vegetables, pancetta and roasted garlic cloves over the eggs. Sprinkle with cheese, fennel, green onions and paprika. Transfer pan to the oven and continue to broil for 5 minutes more or until eggs set. Remove and serve with crusty garlic bread.

INGREDIENTS

1/4 cup (60 mL) olive oil, divided
1/2 cup (125 mL) diced pancetta or smoked ham
1/4 cup (60 mL) diced red bell peppers
1/4 cup (60 mL) diced orange bell peppers
1 cup (250 mL) broccoli florets, cut in half
1 cup (250 mL) cauliflower florets, cut in half
2 large orange-fleshed sweet potatoes, grated
Salt and pepper to taste
1 dozen large eggs
1/4 cup (60 mL) half-and-half cream (10%)
1 head garlic, roasted (remove cloves)
1/4 cup (60 mL) grated Parmesan cheese
1 tsp (5 mL) fennel seeds, toasted, ground
1/4 cup (60 mL) green onions, thinly sliced on the diagonal
1/4 tsp (1 mL) smoked paprika

Crème de Banana Stuffed-French Toast

Crème de Banana happens to be one my favorite liqueurs, so it's not a coincidence that I made it a primary component in this recipe. Enjoy it with a Yellow Bird cocktail. After all, who says you can't have a cocktail at brunch?

Serves 4

1. To prepare the crème de banana sauce, place dulce de leche and liqueur in the bowl of a food processor and purée. Set aside

2. To prepare the banana filling, in a skillet, combine bananas and liqueur over medium heat and toss to coat. Add cream cheese to pan and fold in banana mixture. Cook for 1 minute. Remove from heat and set aside.

3. To prepare the French toast, in a medium bowl, crack eggs and slowly add cream while whisking. Add salt, cinnamon, nutmeg and vanilla and whisk well.

4. To assemble the French toast, in a large skillet, heat 3 Tbsp (45 mL) butter over medium heat.

5. Spread cream cheese filling generously over 1 slice of bread. Place sliced banana filling on top and cover with another slice of bread using cream cheese as the glue to seal edges together.

6. Dip bread in egg batter and flip over with a spatula to coat the other side. Transfer to the skillet and fry until golden on one side, then flip over to fry the other side, about 3 minutes per side.

7. Transfer to a plate and keep warm in the oven. Repeat with remaining bread slices.

8. To serve, drizzle the Crème de Banana Sauce on a plate, cut sandwich in half on the diagonal and set on the plate. Drizzle with sauce again, garnish with coconut flakes, hazelnut, sugar, lime zest and chocolate shavings. Repeat with remaining slices and indulge!

INGREDIENTS

1 cup (250 mL) Prepared Dulce de Leche, (see recipe on page 17)

Crème de Banana Sauce
1 cup (250 mL) dulce de leche
1 Tbsp (15 mL) crème de banana liqueur

Banana Filling
3 ripe bananas, sliced
1/4 cup (60 mL) crème de banana liqueur
1 cup (250 mL) cream cheese, softened

French Toast
4 large eggs
1/4 cup (60 mL) half-and-half cream (10%)
1/4 tsp (1 mL) salt
1/2 tsp (2 mL) ground cinnamon
1/4 tsp (1 mL) ground nutmeg
1 tsp (5 mL) pure vanilla extract
1/2 cup (125 mL) butter, divided
8 thick slices coconut or brioche bread

Garnish
1/2 cup (125 mL) unsweetened toasted coconut flakes
1/2 cup (125 mL) toasted hazelnut pieces
1 Tbsp (15 mL) confectioner's (icing) sugar
Zest of 3 limes
1 cup (250 mL) chocolate shavings

CHAPTER 3

COMFORTING *Soups*

- SAVORY COCONUT CURRY SOUP

- CONCH CHILI WITH BEER

- ANDROS CRAB SOUP

- STEW CHICKEN

- GRAND BAHAMA CONCH CHOWDER
  WITH KAFFIR LIME ESSENCE

- SPICY TURKEY CHILI

- FARMERS MARKET VEGETABLE SOUP

- HARVEST PUMPKIN SOUP

- SMOKED FISH & CORN CHOWDER

- CAT ISLAND OKRA SOUP

- PIGEON PEAS & DUMPLING SOUP

- AUNT LULA'S "SHUT UP & EAT"
  WHITE BEAN SOUP

- LEMONY CHICKEN NOODLE SOUP

- DOWN-HOME CHICKEN &
  DUMPLING SOUP

- LEMONGRASS & CELERIAC SOUP

- SMOKED SALMON CHOWDER

- SWEET FIELD CORN & CRAB SOUP

SAVORY COCONUT CURRY SOUP

This soup is great as a starter and will impress your guests every time. You may add shrimp, fish or chicken to this recipe when preparing as a main course. Serve with Exotic Chips (see recipe, page 16).

Serves 4

1. In a 6-quart (6 L) pot, heat oil over medium heat. Add lemongrass, minced ginger and curry powder and cook, stirring, until fragrant, about 1–2 minutes.
2. Stir in coconut milk, stock and sugar. Increase heat to high and bring to a boil. Reduce heat and simmer, stirring occasionally, for 30 minutes or until slightly thickened.
3. Season to taste with salt and pepper. Add fresh basil leaves and continue to simmer for 5 minutes more.
4. Garnish with peppers, green onions and Cumin Crème.

TIP: Soups are great for entertaining guests, as the flavor enhances each day for up to a week in the refrigerator when stored properly in an airtight container. Store in the freezer and it will last for a month. Always thaw frozen soups overnight in the refrigerator. Another process for thawing soups is to store them in vacuum sealed food-safe bags by placing the bag inside a pot of water (with enough water to cover) and bringing it up to a boil; when the soup has thawed, open the bag and pour the soup into another pot. Let the soup simmer until heated through while stirring and serve at once.

INGREDIENTS

2 Tbsp (30 mL) olive oil
2 tsp (10 mL) lemongrass paste
2 tsp (10 mL) minced fresh ginger
2 Tbsp (30 mL) Caribbean curry powder
3 cups (750 mL)) coconut milk
2 cups (500 mL) chicken stock
2 Tbsp (30 mL) light brown sugar
2 Tbsp (30 mL) fine sea salt
1/4 tsp (1 mL) white pepper
1 Tbsp (15 mL) fresh basil leaves, chiffonade

Garnish

4 cherry peppers, seeds removed and diced
1/2 bunch green onions, thinly sliced on the diagonal
1 cup (250 mL) Cumin Crème (see recipe, page 3)

Conch Chili with Beer

Conch (pronounced "konk") is The Bahamas quintessential treasure of the sea. It's a mollusk that has a mild, sweet flavor that is similar in taste to clams. Queen conchs achieve full size at about 3 to 5 years of age, can grow to a maximum of 12 inches (30 cm) long and weigh up to 5 lbs (2.2 kg).

Serves 8

1. To prepare the conch, follow recipe to tenderize conchs on page 19.
2. Cut meat into 1-inch (2.5 cm) pieces and place in the bowl of a food processor or meat grinder and pulse until pea size. Set aside.
3. In an 8-quart (8 L) pot, heat oil over medium heat. Add onion and sweat onion until translucent, about 3 minutes.
4. Add green and red bell peppers, celery, garlic and tomatoes and cook, stirring, for 3 minutes.
5. Add beer and reduce by half.
6. Add conch and 1 cup (250 mL) of the reserved stock and stir.
7. Add remaining ingredients (except garnish) and bring chili to a boil. Reduce heat and simmer, stirring occasionally, for 45 minutes.
8. Season to taste with salt and pepper. Garnish with sour cream and green onions and serve with a side of Native Cornbread (if desired).

INGREDIENTS

1 lb (450 kg) ground conch meat
3 Tbsp (45 mL) olive oil
1 large onion, diced
1/2 green bell pepper, diced
1/2 red bell pepper, diced
2 stalks celery, diced
4 cloves garlic, diced
3 cups (750 mL) diced tomatoes
1 cup (250 mL) beer
1 cup (250 mL) reserved conch stock
3 cups (750 mL) red kidney
  beans, cooked
1 tsp (5 mL) dried oregano
2 tsp (10 mL) fresh thyme leaves
1 tsp (5 mL) ground cumin
1 Tbsp (15 mL) brown sugar
1 Scotch bonnet pepper, diced
1 Tbsp (15 mL) chili powder
Salt and pepper to taste

Garnish

1 cup (250 mL) sour cream
1/4 bunch green onions, thinly sliced on
  the diagonal

Native Skillet Cornbread (see recipe,
  page 36) (optional)

ANDROS CRAB SOUP

Andros is the largest island in the Bahamas at 2,300 square miles (3,700 square km) in size. The island is known for its famous blue holes (underwater cave systems). It is also referred to as "The Land of Crabs." The annual All Andros Crab Festival occurs around the middle of June, so if you're a crab lover here's an opportunity to experience an abundance of scrumptious crab recipes.

Serves 8

1. In an 8-quart (8 L) pot, heat coconut oil over medium heat. Add salted pork and render fat until crisp, about 3 minutes.
2. Add onions, celery and carrots and cook, stirring, for 3 minutes.
3. Add flour and cook, stirring, until color changes to brown to make a roux.
4. Add tomato paste and stir for 3 minutes more. Add pigeon peas, biters and legs.
5. Add stock and more water to cover. Bring up to a boil. Reduce heat and simmer.
6. Stir in browning. Add potatoes, cassava, corn, thyme, oregano and parsley and continue cooking for 15 minutes.
7. Stir in lump crabmeat. Add dumplings and cook for 15 minutes.
8. Season to taste with salt and pepper. Add pepper sauce and cook for 5 minutes.

TIP: The primary ingredient in this soup is Andros' white land crabs. However, these crabs are not accessible worldwide so substitute with your favorite hard shell small crabs.

INGREDIENTS

3 Tbsp (45 mL) coconut oil

4 1/2 oz (125 g) salted pork, diced

1 onion, thinly sliced

2 stalks celery, diced

2 carrots, diced

2 Tbsp (30 mL) all-purpose flour

2 Tbsp (30 mL) tomato paste

1 cup (250 mL) canned pigeon peas, drained and rinsed

1 1/2 lbs (750 g) crab biters and legs

4 cups (1 L) seafood stock

2 tsp (10 mL) browning (see page 219)

2 Caribbean sweet potatoes, diced

1 cassava, diced

2 ears corn, husk discarded, cut into 8 pieces

1 tsp (5 mL) fresh thyme leaves

1 tsp (5 mL) dried oregano

1 Tbsp (15 mL) chopped fresh Italian parsley

4 cups (1 L) lump crabmeat

1/2 lb (225 g) Homemade Dumplings (see Variation, page 15)

Salt and pepper to taste

2 Tbsp (30 mL) Bahamian Pepper Sauce (see recipe, page 3)

Stew Chicken

Be prepared to take a "power nap" after eating a bowl of this rich and savory stew. Perfect for brunch with an ice-cold beer.

Serves 6

1. Place white vinegar in a large bowl of water and rinse chicken wings. Drain and pat dry with paper towels.
2. Pour red wine vinegar over the chicken and season with seasoned salt.
3. In a skillet, add 1/2 cup (125 mL) of the oil over medium heat. Brown chicken on both sides. Set aside on a plate.
4. In an 8-quart (8 L) pot, add remaining oil over medium heat. Stir in flour to make a dark brown roux. Add paste and continue to stir.
5. Add onion and celery and cook for 2 minutes. Add tomatoes and cook, stirring, for 2 minutes more.
6. Add chicken stock, stirring occasionally, and bring to a boil. Add chicken (along with any juices in the bowl), potato, carrot, bay leaf and thyme. Reduce heat and simmer, covered with a lid that's slightly ajar and cook, about 40 minutes or until chicken is well done. The soup should thicken slightly to coat the back of a spoon.
7. Add parsley and pepper sauce (if using). Season with salt and pepper to taste and cook for 5 minutes more. Serve at once.

INGREDIENTS

1 Tbsp (15 mL) white vinegar

3 lbs (1.4 kg) chicken wings including drumettes (separated)

1 cup (250 mL) red wine vinegar

1/4 cup (60 mL) Raquel's Seasoned Salt (see recipe, page 2)

1 cup (250 mL) vegetable oil, divided

2/3 cup (160 mL) all-purpose flour

1 tsp (5 mL) tomato paste

1/2 medium onion, sliced thinly

2 stalks celery, diced

1 cup (250 mL) fire-roasted diced tomatoes

8 cups (2 L) chicken stock

1 Caribbean sweet potato, diced

1 large carrot, diced

1 bay leaf

1 tsp (5 mL) fresh thyme leaves

2 Tbsp 30 mL) diced fresh Italian parsley

2 Tbsp (30 mL) Bahamian Pepper Sauce (see recipe, page 3) (optional)

Salt and pepper to taste

GRAND BAHAMA CONCH CHOWDER WITH KAFFIR LIME ESSENCE

Throughout The Bahamas this is most requested soup. It's served with a side of Sherry-Pepper Vinegar, and you should anticipate the senses being awakened with the aroma of this delectable legendary conch chowder. It's fully loaded with tender morsels of conch, vegetables, herbs and spices, and—for the finale—a warm slice of buttery light and fluffy johnny cake.

Serves 8

1. To prepare the sherry pepper vinegar, in a small 1.5-quart (1.5 L) saucepan, heat vinegar, Scotch bonnet pepper and thyme sprigs over medium heat. Bring to a boil. Reduce heat and simmer for 10–15 minutes.
2. Strain vinegar and discard pepper and thyme. Let cool and store in a sterilized jar.
3. Follow recipe for tenderizing conchs on page 18, reserving the flavorful stock.
4. Dice conchs and season with seasoned salt. Set aside.
5. In an 8-quart (8 L) pot, heat oil over medium heat. Add onion, celery, bell pepper, garlic and thyme and cook for 3 minutes.
6. Stir in tomato paste. Add tomatoes and cook for 3 minutes more.
7. Add reserved stock and bring to a boil. Add lime leaves, potato, carrots and conch. Reduce heat and simmer for 30 minutes.
8. Add Worcestershire sauce, basil and parsley. Season to taste with salt and pepper and simmer for 5 minutes more. Serve with sherry vinegar and a slice of johnny cake.

TIP: For a neat presentation, serve the sherry vinegar in shot glasses as an accompaniment to the chowder.

INGREDIENTS

Sherry Pepper Vinegar
1 cup (250 mL) sherry vinegar
1 Scotch bonnet pepper, cut in half
3 sprigs thyme

4 Queen conchs
1 Tbsp (15 mL) Raquel's Seasoned Salt (see recipe, page 2)
3 Tbsp (45 mL) olive oil
1/2 sweet onion, diced
2 stalks celery, finely diced
1/2 green bell pepper, finely diced
6 cloves garlic, finely diced
1 tsp (5 mL) fresh thyme leaves
1 Tbsp (15 mL) tomato paste
2 cups (500 mL) diced tomatoes
2 kaffir lime leaves
1 russet potato, diced
2 Caribbean sweet potatoes, diced
2 carrots, diced
1 Tbsp (15 mL) Worcestershire sauce
2 fresh basil leaves, chiffonade
1 Tbsp (15 mL) chopped fresh Italian parsley
Fine sea salt and pepper to taste
Aunt Tia's Coconut Johnny Cake (see recipe, page 34) (optional)

Spicy Turkey Chili

Bahamians absolutely love flavorful spices. Our cuisine is never bland and this chili is a great example of this fact.

Serves 8

1. To prepare the poblano peppers, use a tong to place peppers over an open flame and char until black on all sides. Place peppers in a bowl covered with plastic wrap for 3 minutes. Remove the charred skin by rubbing it off with your hands. Dice peppers and set aside.

2. In a skillet over medium heat, add half of the oil. Add turkey and cook, breaking up the pieces, about 5 minutes. Drain and set aside.

3. In an 8-quart (8 L) pot, heat remaining oil over medium heat. Add onion and sweat until translucent, about 3 minutes.

4. Add garlic, bell pepper, Poblano peppers and tomatoes and continue to cook for 3 minutes.

5. Add remaining ingredients (except the Cumin Crème) and continue cooking until chili comes to a full boil. Reduce heat and simmer for 15 minutes. Season with salt and pepper to taste and serve with Cumin Crème (if desired) and crackers.

INGREDIENTS

2 poblano peppers
1/3 cup (80 mL) olive oil, divided
2 lbs (1 kg) ground turkey
1 onion, diced
2 Tbsp (30 mL) garlic paste
1/2 green bell pepper, diced
3 cups (750 mL) diced tomatoes
2 cups (500 mL) red kidney beans
1 tsp (5 mL) dried oregano
1 tsp (5 mL) ground cumin
2 tsp (10 mL) brown sugar
2 tsp (10 mL) Raquel's Seasoned Salt
   (see recipe, page 2)
1 Tbsp (15 mL) chili powder
2 Tbsp (30 mL) Worcestershire sauce
Salt and pepper to taste
Cumin Crème (see recipe, page 3)
   (optional)

FARMERS MARKET VEGETABLE SOUP

Fresh is always best so I encourage you to shop at your local farmers' market and add your vegetables of choice to this invigorating soup.

Serves 8

1. In a 6-quart (6 L) pot, heat stock over medium heat. Bring to a boil, then reduce heat and simmer. Keep warm.
2. In an 8-quart (8 L) pot, heat oil over medium heat. Add onion, garlic, celery, red and orange peppers and cook for 3 minutes.
3. Add tomatoes and cook for 3 minutes more. Add stock and bay leaf and bring to a boil. Stir in remaining ingredients. Reduce heat to medium and let cook until vegetables are vibrant in color, about 15–20 minutes.
4. Drizzle with Green Vinaigrette and serve immediately.

INGREDIENTS

8 cups (2 L) vegetable stock
3 Tbsp (45 mL) olive oil
1/2 red onion, sliced
4 cloves garlic, diced
2 stalks celery, diced
1/2 red bell pepper, diced
1/2 orange bell pepper, diced
1 1/2 cups (375 mL) diced fire-roasted
   tomatoes
1 bay leaf
1 cup (250 mL) shredded savoy cabbage
1 cup (250 mL) shredded red cabbage
2 cups (500 mL) torn callaloo leaves
1/4 lb (110 g) fresh green beans,
   cut in half
3 ears corn, cooked and kernels removed
2 large carrots, sliced
1 Tbsp (15 mL) fresh basil leaves,
   chiffonade
1 Tbsp (15 mL) Italian seasoning
Salt and pepper to taste
1 cup (250 mL) Green Vinaigrette (see
   recipe, page 4)

HARVEST PUMPKIN SOUP

It's harvest time again! My grandfather was a farmer and pumpkin was one of the many fruits that grew on our land. I was fortunate to experience the joys of watching produce grow from a seed to maturity to harvesting and then to the dinner table.

Serves 10

1. Preheat oven to 300°F (150°C). Line a baking sheet with parchment paper. Cut pumpkin into 4 pieces. Remove seeds with a spoon and clean. Transfer seeds to a small bowl.

2. In a bowl, toss pumpkin seeds with salt and pepper to taste, cumin and 1 Tbsp (15 mL) of the olive oil. Spread seeds in a single layer on the baking sheet and bake for 30 minutes until golden. Set aside.

3. Line another baking sheet with parchment paper. Place pumpkin, skin side down, on the baking sheet. Drizzle with 3 Tbsp (45 mL) of oil and season to taste with salt and pepper. Roast pumpkin in the oven with seeds until tender when pierced with a knife (a total of about 90 minutes for the pumpkin). Remove pumpkin seeds after 30 minutes. Increase oven temperature to 400°F (200°C) and continue baking the pumpkin, about 60 minutes more. Remove from the oven and let cool. Peel the skin with a sharp knife and discard. Dice pumpkin and set aside.

4. Meanwhile, in a 6-quart (6 L) pot, bring stock to a boil over medium high heat. Reduce heat to low.

5. Cut off tough green parts from leeks and discard. Slice tender white parts in half and place in a large bowl of cold water. Separate the layers to wash thoroughly as leeks are usually filled with sand. Remove leeks from the bowl. Dry with paper towels and dice.

INGREDIENTS

5 lb (2.2 kg) pumpkin
Salt and pepper
1/4 tsp (1 mL) ground cumin
6 Tbsp (90 mL) olive oil, divided
8 cups (2 L) vegetable stock
2 leeks (white and tender green parts only), rinsed
2 Tbsp (30 mL) butter
2 orange-fleshed sweet potatoes, diced
2 russet potatoes, diced
1 Tbsp (30 mL) light brown sugar
2 tsp (10 mL) freshly grated nutmeg
Salt and white pepper to taste
2 cups (500 mL) crème fraîche, for garnish
1/2 cup (125 mL) toasted pumpkin seeds
1/4 cup (60 mL) Green Vinaigrette (see recipe, page 4)

6. In a skillet, add remaining oil and butter over medium heat. Add leeks and cook for 2 minutes. Add sweet and russet potatoes and cook, stirring occasionally, for 3 minutes more. Transfer vegetables along with pumpkin to an 8-quart (8 L) pot over medium heat and add the hot stock.
7. Using a hand-held immersion blender, carefully purée the vegetables to a smooth consistency that coats the back of a spoon (add water to thin the soup to desired texture).
8. Stir soup and add sugar, nutmeg and season to taste with salt and pepper. Garnish with crème fraîche and sprinkle with toasted pumpkin seeds and green vinaigrette.

TIPS: If you do not have an immersion blender, let the soup cool down, then use a food processor to purée the vegetables with the stock in batches, and return to the pot.

If you have a double oven, set one on 300°F (150°C) to roast the seeds for 30 minutes, and the other oven to 400°F (200°C) to roast the pumpkin for 60 minutes.

Smoked Fish & Corn Chowder

This soup is the ultimate comfort food during the winter months. Smoked fish makes all the difference in this flavorful recipe, and I prefer to use smoked mackerel or herring, which can be purchased at any Caribbean or Asian Market.

Serves 8

1. In a medium skillet, heat oil over medium heat. Add onion and cook until translucent, about 3 minutes. Add garlic and tomatoes and cook for 3 minutes.
2. Add wine and reduce by half. Add sweet potato, red potatoes, corn and stock and bring to a boil. Reduce heat and simmer for 30 minutes.
3. Add fish and let cook for 5 minutes.
4. In a small bowl, combine flour and water and mix to make a slurry to thicken the soup.
5. Add 1 Tbsp (15 mL) of the hot soup to the flour mixture to temper. Then add another 1Tbsp (15 mL). Pour mixture into the soup while stirring and let cook for 10 minutes more.
6. Stir in coconut milk. Add remaining ingredients and cook for 5 minutes. Season to taste and serve.

> **TIP:** To smoke fresh fish preheat oven to 200˚F (95˚C).
>   Place fillets on a wire rack. Soak 4 cups (1 L) flavored wood chips in water for 30 minutes.
>   In the bottom of a deep roasting pan, combine wet wood chips and 4 cups (1 L) dry wood chips. Place foil over the chips and make slits in foil with a paring knife for the hot smoke to escape.
>   Place the wire rack (with the fillets) on the tray over the foil. Smoke in oven for 2 hours or until fish flakes easily when tested with a fork.

INGREDIENTS

3 Tbsp (45 mL) olive oil

1 onion, diced

2 cloves garlic, diced

1 cup (250 mL) diced tomatoes

1 cup (250 mL) white wine

1 Jamaican sweet potato, cut into 1-inch (2.5 cm) pieces (see page 223)

1/2 lb (225 g) small red potatoes, cut into quarter pieces

2 ears corn, cooked and kernels removed

8 cups (2 L) fish stock

1 lb (450 g) smoked mackerel or herring, deboned

2 Tbsp (30 mL) all-purpose flour

1/4 cup (60 mL) water

1 cup (250 mL) coconut milk

6 slices smoked bacon, cooked and crumbled

1/2 tsp (2 mL) smoked paprika

1 tsp (5 mL) dried oregano

2 tsp (10 mL) diced fresh Italian parsley

Salt and white pepper to taste

CAT ISLAND OKRA SOUP

If you love gumbo, you'll certainly appreciate the taste of okra in this savory and piquant soup. Okra is known in some countries as ladies' fingers due to its shape. It's valued for its edible green seed pods that exude a mucilaginous juice that is perfect for thickening soups and stews.

Serves 8

1. In a 7-quart (7 L) Dutch oven, add oxtails, ham hock and salted beef and cover with water. Place pot over medium-high heat and bring to a boil. Reduce heat and cover and simmer for 60 minutes.
2. In an 8-quart (8 L) pot, heat oil over medium heat. Add okra and cook, stirring occasionally, for 5 minutes. Add onion, celery and garlic and cook for 3 minutes.
3. Add stock and bring to a boil. Add meats. Reduce heat and simmer, stirring occasionally, for 30 minutes.
4. Add remaining ingredients and cook for 30 minutes more. Serve over rice.

INGREDIENTS

2 lbs (1 kg) oxtails cut into 1 inch (2.5 cm) pieces
1 lb (450 kg) smoked ham hock
1 lb (450 kg) salted beef, cut into 1-inch (2.5 cm) pieces
Water
3 Tbsp (45 mL) olive oil
2 lbs (1 kg) fresh or frozen okra, diced
1 onion, diced
2 stalks celery, diced
4 cloves garlic, finely diced
8 cups (2 L) beef stock
1 tsp (5 mL) dried thyme leaves
1 bay leaf
2 tsp (10 mL) Italian seasoning
1 Scotch bonnet pepper, finely diced
2 tsp (10 mL) browning (see page 219)
Salt and pepper to taste
Cooked rice

Pigeon Peas & Dumpling Soup

Pigeon peas are green in the pod when young and could be enjoyed as a snack or in salads for a nutty flavor. Dried pigeon peas are the key ingredient in this soup for an earthy flavor and brown color. They should be soaked overnight for easy digestion and a shorter cooking time.

Serves 8

1. In a 4-quart (4 L) Dutch oven, add ham and salted beef and cover with water. Place pot over high heat and bring to a boil; scald meat for 10 minutes. Discard the water.

2. Return pot with meat over medium heat, add peas and cover with water again. Add 1 diced onion, celery and bay leaf and bring to a boil. Reduce heat and simmer for 60 minutes.

3. Remove meat. When cool enough to handle cut meat away from the bone and set aside. Drain peas and set aside. Reserve the flavorful stock and discard the vegetables.

4. In the bowl of a food processor, purée half of the peas and 2 cups (500 mL) of reserved stock. Set aside.

5. In an 8-quart (8 L) pot, heat oil over medium heat. Add 1/2 diced onion and garlic and cook, stirring, for 3 minutes.

6. Add potatoes and remaining reserved stock and bring to a boil. Add meats, whole and puréed peas and more water to cover by 1 inch (2.5 cm). Reduce heat and simmer for 30 minutes.

7. Add dumplings and remaining ingredients and let cook for 15 minutes more. Serve at once.

INGREDIENTS

2 smoked ham hocks (each 10 oz/300 g)
2 lbs (1 kg) salted beef, cut into 1-inch (2.5 cm) pieces
Water
2 cups (500 mL) dried pigeon peas (soaked in water overnight)
1 1/2 onions, diced, divided
1 stalk celery with leaves, cut in half crosswise
1 bay leaf
3 Tbsp (45 mL) canola oil
4 cloves garlic, diced
2 Caribbean sweet potatoes, diced
1/2 lb (225 g) Homemade Dumplings (see recipe, page 15)
2 tsp (10 mL) browning (see Tip, page 219)
1 tsp (5 mL) fresh thyme leaves
1 tsp (5 mL) Italian seasoning
1 Scotch bonnet pepper, finely diced
Salt and pepper to taste

Aunt Lula's "Shut Up & Eat" White Bean Soup

If I had to choose my favorite soup . . . this would be it! It's a versatile soup where you may use seafood, beef, poultry or omit the meat and enjoy as a vegetable soup. It's the mother of all soups. It's ambrosial, hearty and rich, so set aside your deep soup bowls and prepare to be wowed by my aunt's legendary soup.
Serves 12

1. Soak beans overnight in a large bowl. Shell the beans, discarding the outer layer, and set aside in a medium bowl.
2. In a large 8-quart (8 L) pot, combine the meats (except for the wings) and cover with water. Place the pot over high heat and bring to a boil. Reduce heat and simmer for 1 hour.
3. Drain the greasy broth and transfer the meats, turkey and beans to a 10-quart (10 L) pot. Add water to cover the meats by 2 inches (5 cm). Place the pot over medium-high heat, cover with the lid slightly ajar and bring to a boil.
4. Remove the lid and add onion, celery, garlic, bay leaf and tomatoes. Reduce heat to medium, cover slightly ajar to let out steam and cook, stirring occasionally, for 45 minutes.
5. Add all vegetables (except for the plantain), spices and herbs, seasoned salt and Scotch bonnet peppers and cook, stirring occasionally, for 30 minutes.
6. Add dumplings, plantain and ketchup and cook for 15 minutes more.
7. Season to taste with the salt and pepper and serve at once

> **TIPS:** If you're making the seafood version, omit steps 2 and 3, add the beans in step 4, then add the seafood in step 6 and cook until opaque. For a more flavorful broth, let most of the beans dissolve by cooking for 15 minutes more in step 4.
> To cut up wings, use a sharp knife or ask your butcher to do it.

INGREDIENTS

4 cups (1 L) dried large white lima beans
1/2 lb (225 g) oxtails
1 lb (450 kg) smoked ham hock
1/2 lb (225 g) pickled or smoked pork tails
1/2 lb (225 g) salted beef, cut into 1-inch (2.5 cm) pieces
1/2 lb (225 g) tenderized conch meat, cut into 1-inch (2.5 cm) pieces
1/2 lb (225 g) smoked turkey wings, cut into 1-inch (2.5 cm) pieces
1/2 onion, sliced
2 stalks celery, diced
8 cloves garlic, diced
1 bay leaf
2 cups (500 mL) diced tomatoes
3 ears corn, husk discarded, cut into 9 pieces
1 orange-fleshed sweet potato, diced
1 Caribbean sweet potato, diced
1 eddoes, diced
1 cassava (yuca), cut into 1-inch (2.5 cm) pieces
2 large carrots, sliced
2 tsp (10 mL) dried oregano
1 Tbsp (15 mL) Italian seasoning
2 tsp (10 mL) dried parsley flakes
1 tsp (5 mL) fresh thyme leaves
1 Tbsp (15 mL) Raquel's Seasoned Salt (see recipe, page 2)
1 1/2 Scotch bonnet peppers, diced

continued on next page

Salt and pepper to taste
1/2 lb (225 g) Homemade Dumplings (see
   recipe, page 15)
1 large half-ripe plantain, cut into 1-inch
   (2.5 cm) pieces
1/2 cup (125 mL) ketchup

LEMONY CHICKEN NOODLE SOUP

This delicious soup can be enjoyed in any season. Especially when you're feeling a bit "under the weather," this soup will put the pep back in your step!

Serves 6

1. In a 4-quart (4 L) pot, bring stock to a boil over medium heat. Add onion, celery and carrots. Reduce heat and simmer for 10 minutes.
2. Add chicken and remaining ingredients and cook, stirring, for 20 minutes more. Season to taste and serve with lemon wedges.

INGREDIENTS

8 cups (2 L) chicken stock
1/2 onion, thinly sliced
2 stalks celery, diced
2 large carrots, sliced
4 chicken thighs, roasted and shredded
Juice of 3 lemons
1 tsp (5 mL) fresh thyme leaves
1 tsp (5 mL) dried oregano
1/2 tsp (2 mL) ground coriander
1 tsp (5 mL) diced fresh basil
1 tsp (5 mL) diced fresh Italian parsley
1/2 Scotch bonnet pepper, finely diced
1 cup (250 mL) dried egg noodles
Salt and pepper to taste
Lemon wedges

DOWN-HOME CHICKEN & DUMPLING SOUP

"Down-home" is Bahamian jargon for the best unpretentious, hearty and wholesome comfort food. I recommend preparing the flat silky dumplings (see Variation for Flag Dumplings, page 15), for this soup.
Serves 6

1. Rinse chicken and pat dry with paper towels. In a large bowl, combine chicken and vinegar and season each piece with seasoned salt on both sides.
2. In a large skillet, heat oil over medium heat and brown chicken until golden on both sides. Set aside on a plate lined with paper towels.
3. In an 8-quart (8 L) pot, melt butter over medium heat. Add onion, celery and garlic and cook, stirring, for 3 minutes.
4. Add chicken stock, soup and water to cover by 2 inches (5 cm) and bring to a boil. Add chicken. Reduce heat and simmer, covered, stirring occasionally, for 30 minutes.
5. Skim the fat from the surface. Stir in carrots, thyme, oregano and cream and bring to a boil. Add dumplings, one at a time, and reduce heat and simmer for 30 minutes more.
6. In a small bowl, combine flour and 1/4 cup (60 mL) water and mix to make a slurry to thicken the soup.
7. Add 1 Tbsp (15 mL) of the hot soup to the flour mixture to temper, then add another 1 Tbsb (15 mL). Pour mixture into soup while stirring and let cook for 10 minutes more.
8. Add hot pepper sauce and season to taste with salt and pepper. Serve with a side of Native Cornbread.

INGREDIENTS

12 pieces boneless chicken thighs
1 cup (250 mL) red wine vinegar
1/2 cup (125 mL) Raquel's Seasoned
  Salt (see recipe, page 2)
1 cup (250 mL) canola oil
3 Tbsp (45 mL) butter
1 large onion, cut into quarter pieces,
  then in halves
2 stalks celery, cut roughly into 1/2-inch
  (1 cm) pieces
4 cloves garlic, sliced
2 cups (500 mL) cream of chicken soup
8 cups (2 L) chicken stock
Water
4 carrots, cut into 1/2-inch (1 cm) pieces
1/2 tsp (2 mL) fresh thyme leaves
1/2 tsp (2 mL) dried or fresh oregano
1/4 cup (60 mL) whipping (or heavy)
  cream (35%)
1 lb (450 g) Flag Dumplings (see
  Variation, page 15)
2 Tbsp (30 mL) all-purpose flour
1 tsp (5 mL) hot pepper sauce
Salt to taste
1/4 tsp (1 mL) white pepper
Native Skillet Cornbread (see recipe,
  page 36) (optional)

Lemongrass & Celeriac Soup

Lemongrass, which is also known throughout the Bahamas as "fever-grass," is usually boiled, steeped and consumed in tea or broth. Savor the taste in this light, feel-so-good, tea soup.

Serves 6

1. Rinse fish and pat dry with paper towels. Season with seafood seasoning and set aside.
2. Remove the tough outer layers from the lemongrass stalks, and beat a few times with a mallet to release the fragrant oils. Cut 1 stalk in half, finely dice the other stalk and set aside.
3. In a 4-quart (4 L) pot, heat ghee over medium heat. Add diced lemongrass, ginger, leeks and celeriac and cook, stirring, until leeks are tender, about 3 minutes.
4. Add fish stock and water. Add lemongrass stalks and bring to a boil. Reduce heat and simmer for 20 minutes.
5. Add fish, lime juice and Scotch bonnet pepper and cook for 15 minutes more or until fish is opaque. Adjust seasoning, garnish with parsley and serve.

INGREDIENTS

2 red snapper fillets, skin on, cut into 1-inch (2.5 cm) pieces
1 Tbsp (15 mL) seafood seasoning
2 lemongrass stalks
2 Tbsp (30 mL) ghee
1 tsp (5 mL) minced ginger
2 leeks, soaked and rinsed
2 cups (500 mL) celeriac (celery root), peeled and diced
4 cups (1 L) fish or seafood stock
2 cups (500 mL) water
Juice of 2 limes
1/2 Scotch bonnet pepper, finely diced
Salt and pepper to taste
1 Tbsp (15 mL) fresh Italian parsley, for garnish

Smoked Salmon Chowder

A popular item on my former restaurant's (The Wine Lounge) menu that started out as a soup-of-the-day special but, due to demand, became a fixed selection. It was attractively served inside of warm puff pastry shell and garnished with morsels of smoked salmon, crème fraîche, smoked paprika and chives. Divine!

Serves 4

1. Follow directions on the package to bake the puff pastry shells and set aside.
2. In a 4-quart (4 L) pot, heat butter and oil over medium heat. Add onion and garlic and cook, stirring, for 3 minutes.
3. Add potatoes and cook for 3 minutes. Add stock and bring to a boil. Reduce heat and simmer. Add tomato sauce, basil and sugar and cook for 20 minutes.
4. Using a hand-held immersion blender, purée potatoes and thicken the soup.
5. Add cream and continue to simmer for 10 minutes (the soup should be pink in color). Adjust seasoning with salt and pepper.
6. To plate, place 1 puff pastry shell inside a soup bowl. Ladle soup inside and around pastry shell. Place a few slices of smoked salmon in the center of the pastry shell and garnish with a dot of crème fraîche, paprika and chives. Repeat with the other bowls and serve at once.

TIP: To chiffonade the fresh basil, roll the leaves tightly, and thinly slice to make ribbons.

INGREDIENTS

6 puff pastry shells
2 Tbsp (30 mL) butter
1 Tbsp (15 mL) olive oil
1/2 onion, diced
2 garlic cloves, diced
2 yellow-fleshed potatoes, diced
4 cups (1 L) fish stock, heated
2 cups (500 mL) Homemade Tomato Sauce (see recipe, page 8)
1 tsp (5 mL) basil, chiffonade
1 Tbsp (15 mL) light brown sugar
1 cup (250 mL) whipping (or heavy) cream (35%)
Salt and white pepper to taste
2 cups (500 mL) smoked salmon

Garnish
1/2 cup (125 mL) crème fraîche
1/2 tsp (2 mL) smoked paprika
1 Tbsp (15 mL) diced fresh chives

SWEET FIELD CORN & CRAB SOUP

There was always an abundance of fresh ears of corn on our land, so we utilized them in soups, stews, salads and by simply roasting them inside the husk. I must admit that wherever I see a sign that says, "Roasted Corn," I'm pulling the car over. Use fresh farmer's market corn for this soup; it makes all the difference!

Serves 6

1. In a 6-quart (6 L) pot, heat butter and oil over medium heat. Add onion, garlic and bell pepper and cook for 3 minutes.
2. Add wine and reduce by half. Add stock and bring to a boil. Stir in creamed corn and corn kernels. Reduce heat and simmer for 20 minutes.
3. Add crabmeat and remaining ingredients and cook for 10 minutes more. Adjust seasoning and serve with dinner rolls.

INGREDIENTS

2 Tbsp (30 mL) butter
1 Tbsp (15 mL) olive oil
1/2 onion, diced
2 cloves garlic, diced
1/2 red bell pepper, finely diced
1 cup (250 mL) white wine
8 cups (2 L) fish or seafood
   stock, heated
2 cups (500 mL) cream-style corn
3 ears corn, cooked and kernels removed
4 cups (1 L) lump crabmeat, shredded
Juice of 2 lemons
1 Tbsp (15 mL) fish sauce
1 Tbsp (15 mL) finely diced fresh
   Italian parsley
2 fresh basil leaves, diced
Salt and pepper to taste

Downtown Bay Street,
Nassau Paradise Island

CHAPTER 4

BREEZY ISLAND
Starters & Salads

- GUAVA SPICED STUFFED WINGS

- ANDROSIAN STUFFED CRABS

- BACON-WRAPPED PIGEONS (SQUABS) WITH PIKLIZ

- GOLDEN CONCH NIPS

- KONKY CONCH CAKES

- HARBOUR ISLAND LOBSTER SALAD IN CAMPARI CUPS

- GRAND BAHAMA CONCH SALAD

- NASSAU SCORCHED CONCH

- MY BAHAMIAN CONCH FRITTERS

- CARIBBEAN CHICKEN & VEGGIE PATTIES WITH GREEN MANGO CHUTNEY

- CREAMY ROCK LOBSTER MAC 'N' CHEESE

- COD FISH FRITTERS

- SAVORY LAMB TURNOVERS

- TROPICAL FRUIT CHEESE LOG

- PEAR-A-DISE THIN CRUST PIZZA WITH SMOKED DUCK & GOAT CHEESE CRUMBLE

- ABACO STONE CRABS WITH LEMONGRASS & DILL DIPPING SAUCE

- CURRY CHICKEN PIZZA

- TWICE-FRIED PLANTAINS WITH CARIBBEAN MANGO SALSA

- ISLAND CRAB CAKES WRAPPED IN SEAWEED

- TROPICAL MANGO SHRIMP ON LEMONGRASS SKEWERS

- BIMINI COCONUT CRACKED LOBSTER BITES

- STEAMED HAMBURGER SLIDERS WITH ISLAND CURRANT KETCHUP

- TAMARIND CHICKPEA DIP WITH MAMEY CREMA

- GREAT INAGUA CRAB SALAD MELTS

- EXOTIC COLESLAW

- LADY PAT'S AWARD-WINNING POTATO SALAD

- NATIVE CORN & CHARRED PEPPER SALAD

- VANGIE'S BROCCOFLOWER SALAD

- VANGIE'S DELICIOUS LAYERED SALAD

- TANGY MACARONI SALAD

- SPINACH, HIBISCUS & CRABAPPLE SALAD WITH CREAMY SOURSOP-PEPPERCORN DRESSING

- BAHAMA SUMMER RICE SALAD

- DRUM "BEET" SALAD

Guava Spiced Stuffed Wings

Guavas are widely used throughout The Bahamas in sauces, desserts and refreshing drinks. I prefer to use the pink-fleshed guavas as the flavor is sweeter and more prominent than the white-fleshed ones. This fruit has a unique and delightful taste. You may find fresh and canned guavas in your local supermarkets (including guava paste). I decorate the centerpieces in my home with guavas during the summer months for an intoxicating fragrance that lingers throughout the house.

Serves 4

1. Preheat the oven to 350°F (180°C)
2. To prepare the wings for stuffing, cut the drumettes from the wing portion of the chicken and save for another recipe. The wing portion should still be attached to the tip portion of the wing.
3. Using a sharp paring knife, create a pocket by cutting under the skin (close to the bone) in a circular motion around the wing to release the meat and tendons from the bone.
4. Scrape or pull the skin and meat back with the knife, twist and separate the 2 bones from the joint connected at the tip and discard the bones. Now you should have a boneless pocket to fill with the stuffing.
5. Line a baking sheet with parchment paper. Place wings in single rows on the sheet. Drizzle dressing over top and season sparsely with seasoned salt. Set aside.
6. To prepare the stuffing, in a medium skillet, heat olive oil over medium heat. Add sausage and chicken hearts (or gizzards), and cook while separating the pieces, about 10 minutes. Drain and set aside in a small bowl.
7. In a small skillet, toast fennel seeds over low heat until

ingredients continued on page 84

INGREDIENTS

2 lbs (1 kg) chicken wings

Stuffing
1/4 cup (60 mL) Italian salad oil dressing
1/4 cup (60 mL) Raquel's Seasoned Salt (see recipe, page 2)
3 Tbsp (45 mL) olive oil
2 cups (500 mL) ground Italian sausage
1/2 cup (125 mL) finely diced chicken hearts or gizzards
1 tsp (5 mL) fennel seeds
1/4 cup (60 mL) butter
1/2 medium onion, finely diced
3 cloves garlic, finely diced
1/4 piece green bell pepper, finely diced
1 tsp (5 mL) fresh thyme leaves
1 tsp (5 mL) diced fresh Italian parsley
1 cup (250 mL) diced apricots
1 cup (250 mL) plain bread crumbs
1/2 cup (125 mL) panko bread crumbs
1 large egg, slightly beaten
1 tsp (5 mL) lemon zest
Juice of 1 lemon
1/2 cup (125 mL) chicken stock
Salt and pepper to taste

ingredients continued on page 84

fragrant. Set aside on a small plate and let cool, then grind seeds in a spice or coffee grinder.

8. Add butter to the skillet and melt. Add onion, garlic and bell pepper and cook for 3 minutes.

9. In a large bowl, combine meats, cooked vegetables, fennel, thyme, parsley, apricots, bread crumbs, eggs, lemon zest and juice and stock and mix thoroughly. Adjust seasoning.

10. Use a piping bag to stuff each wing with the sausage filling. Pull the skin over the stuffing and cap with the additional meat and skin on the end to seal.

11. To prepare the sauce, in a small saucepan, add paste and water over medium heat and combine thoroughly to make a sauce that coats the back of the spoon. Stir and let simmer for 5 minutes.

12. Reduce heat to low and add remaining ingredients. Stir and let simmer for 5 minutes.

13. Brush or spoon the sauce over the wings, place baking sheet in the oven and bake, about 30–45 minutes.

TIP: Serve wings with a medley of celery, cherry tomatoes and carrot sticks.

Sauce

2 cups (500 mL) guava paste
1/2 cup (125mL) water
1/2 tsp (2 mL) ground cinnamon
1/2 tsp (2 mL) ground thyme
1/4 tsp (1 mL) freshly ground
   black pepper
1 Tbsp (15 mL) sambal oelek
1/4 cup (60 mL) spiced rum

ANDROSIAN STUFFED CRABS

My grandmother originated from the Island of Andros (land of the crabs). She was very skillful at catching live crabs and cleaning out their guts before cooking them for her family. She fed the crabs a diet of coconut for several weeks, so their meat would take on the subtle sweet and nutty flavor. That's what I call cooking with love!

Serves 6

1. Preheat oven to 375°F (190°C).
2. Fill a 6-quart (6 L) pot with water halfway over medium-high heat. Add hard-shell crabs and cook for 20 minutes. Let cool.
3. Separate the crabs back from the body by pulling apart at the center. Remove the yellowish fat from the crabs back (and reserve), being careful not to break the bitter gall bladder bag (a small sack usually hidden under the fat that stores bile). Discard the gall bag. Set aside the crab's back for the stuffing.
4. Pick the meat from the body and claws of the crab and set aside. In a large bowl, combine all crabmeat and add lemon juice and seafood seasoning.
5. In a large skillet, melt butter over medium heat. Add onion, garlic purée, green and red bell peppers and cook for 3 minutes.
6. Add crab fat and meat, thyme, Scotch bonnet pepper and parsley and continue cooking, stirring, for 5 minutes. Add raisins, bread crumbs, stock and salt and pepper to taste and mix thoroughly.
7. Line a baking sheet with parchment paper. Pack stuffing into the crabs' backs and dot with butter. Place on the baking sheet and bake in the oven for 15 minutes or until golden.

INGREDIENTS

6 medium hard-shell crabs
2 cups (500 mL) crab claw meat, picked clean of shell (about 18 oz/510 g), or 1 can (1 lb/450 g) crab claw meat, drained
Juice of 1 lemon
1 Tbsp (15 mL) seafood seasoning
1/4 cup (60 mL) butter
1 onion, finely diced
1 Tbsp (15 mL) store-bought roasted garlic purée
1/4 piece green bell pepper, finely diced
1/4 piece red bell pepper, finely diced
6 sprigs fresh thyme leaves
1/2 Scotch bonnet pepper
1 Tbsp (15 mL) diced fresh Italian parsley
1/2 cup (125 mL) golden raisins
1 cup (250 mL) plain bread crumbs
1 cup (250 mL) panko bread crumbs
1 cup (250 mL) fish or seafood stock
Salt and pepper to taste
Butter

BACON-WRAPPED PIGEONS (SQUABS) WITH PIKLIZ

Pikliz is a Haitian condiment that is used to complement meats and rice. It's a pickled and fermented product and when canned properly, it's a wonderful gift for your guests. Pigeons, quails and pheasants are available in specialty butcher shops or exotic meat markets. They are perfect appetizer portions. Their meat is dark and lean with a gamy flavor that is complemented by the pikliz in this recipe.

Serves 8 as an appetizer

1. Preheat oven to 350°F (180°C). Rinse poultry in a large bowl with water and white vinegar. Pat dry with paper towels.
2. Return poultry to the bowl. Add red wine vinegar, spices and seasoned salt and mix. Rub on both sides of the poultry.
3. Wrap 1 slice of bacon around each poultry segment, making sure to tuck in ends securely.
4. Place the poultry in a 13- x 9-inch (33 x 23 cm) baking dish. Bake in the oven for 30 minutes or until an instant-read thermometer inserted in the center of the meat registers an internal temperature of 165°F (74°C).
5. In another large bowl, prepare the pikliz by adding all remaining ingredients (except for the vinegar), then tossing.
6. Place vegetable mixture in sterilized jars. Pour in white vinegar to cover and seal with lids.
7. Serve bacon-wrapped poultry, topped with pikliz.

TIP: Prepare pikliz a day ahead as the flavor is better the longer it sits and ferments in a cool dry place. After opening, store in the refrigerator for up to 3 weeks.

INGREDIENTS

2 pigeons (squabs), cut into quarter pieces
1 Tbsp (15 mL) white vinegar
1/2 cup (125 mL) red wine vinegar
1/4 cup (60 mL) Raquel's Seasoned Salt (see recipe, page 2)
1 tsp (5 mL) dried oregano
1 sprig rosemary
8 slices smoked bacon
3 Tbsp (45 mL) olive oil

Pikliz

1/2 head green cabbage, finely grated
1/4 head red cabbage, finely grated
1 carrot, finely grated
Juice of 1 lime
2 Scotch bonnet peppers, finely diced
2 shallots, diced
6 cloves garlic, diced
1 Tbsp (15 mL) allspice berries
1 head garlic, cloves diced
1 tsp (5 mL) fine sea salt
White vinegar (to cover)

Golden Conch Nips

Enjoy these perfectly golden blissful bites of deep-fried tender conch.

Serves 4

1. Preheat a deep fryer with oil to 350°F (180°C).
2. Cut tenderized conchs into 1-inch (2.5 cm) bite-size pieces. Place in a small bowl and season with seasoned salt. Set aside.
3. To prepare the batter, in a medium bowl, add eggs and whisk while pouring in buttermilk. Add 2 cups (500 mL) of the flour and continue whisking to make a smooth batter. Season to taste with salt and pepper.
4. Add remaining flour to a large food storage bag with 1/4 tsp (1 mL) black pepper and shake bag to mix. Set aside.
5. Add conch pieces to batter (1 cup/250 mL at a time), and use a slotted spoon to remove nips. Transfer to bag with flour and shake rigorously to coat.
6. Place conch nips in the fryer basket and fry until golden. Transfer to a plate lined with paper towels. Repeat with remaining pieces and serve immediately with GoomBay Sauce.

TIP: If you don't have a deep fryer, use a wok or a deep 4-quart (4 L) pot. Add 3 inches (8 cm) oil and heat to 350°F (180°C). (Attach a clip-on frying thermometer to gauge heat.) Do not overcrowd the pot with more than 1 cup (250 mL) of the conch nips as it will reduce the temperature of the oil. Use a spider or slotted spoon to remove the golden nips from the oil.

INGREDIENTS

Canola or vegetable oil
4 Queen conchs, tenderized (see method, page 18)
2 Tbsp (30 mL) Raquel's Seasoned Salt (see recipe, page 2)
1 cup (250 mL) Raquel's GoomBay Sauce (see recipe, page 5)

Batter

2 large eggs
2 cups (500 mL) buttermilk
4 cups (1 L) all-purpose flour, divided
1/4 tsp (1 mL) salt
1/4 tsp (1 mL) freshly ground black pepper

KONKY CONCH CAKES

These cakes are a gastronomical delight! They're great accompanied with my GoomBay Sauce or Guava Bell Pepper Jam. Try these cakes as delectable sliders with your favorite toppings and condiments.
Serves 6

1. To prepare the conch cakes, cut conchs into 1-inch (2.5 cm) pieces. In the bowl of a food processor, add 2 cups (500 mL) of conchs at a time with 1/4 cup (60 mL) of the reserved stock and grind into lentil-size pieces. Repeat with remaining conch meat.
2. Place meat in a large bowl and season with seasoned salt. Mix well.
3. Add garlic, onions, bell pepper, mayonnaise and mustard and mix.
4. Add lime juice, bread crumbs, eggs, thyme, parsley, pepper sauce, oregano, paprika and salt and pepper and mix well. (If the first conch cake is too soft add a little more panko into the bowl and mix.)
5. Line a baking sheet with parchment paper. Scoop 2 Tbsp (30 mL) of the conch mixture and form into cakes. Repeat with remaining mixture and place on the baking sheet.
6. In a large skillet, heat oil over medium heat. Dust cakes with flour on both sides and fry until golden, about 3 minutes per side, then turn over with a spatula. Keep warm in the oven. Serve over a bed of Exotic Coleslaw with GoomBay Sauce and Guava Bell Pepper Jam.

Tip: To bake the cakes in the oven, preheat to 400°F (200°C). In a large ovenproof skillet, heat 2 Tbsp (30 mL) canola over medium heat (making sure the bottom of the pan is covered). When oil is hot, add cakes. Fry cakes until golden, about 2 minutes, turn them over with a spatula and fry for 1 minute: transfer to the oven until the cakes cook through, about 5–10 minutes.

INGREDIENTS

2 lbs (1 kg) conch meat, tenderized (see method, page 18)
1 cup (250 mL) reserved conch stock
3 Tbsp (45 mL) Raquel's Seasoned Salt (see recipe, page 2)
4 cloves garlic, diced
1/2 cup (125 mL) onions, diced
1/4 cup (60 mL) diced red bell pepper
1 cup (250 mL) mayonnaise
2 tsp (10 mL) Dijon mustard
1/2 cup (125 mL) lime juice
4 cups (1 L) plain bread crumbs
1 cup (250 mL) panko bread crumbs
2 eggs, slightly beaten
2 tsp (10 mL) fresh thyme leaves
1 Tbsp (15 mL) diced fresh Italian parsley
2 tsp (10 mL) Caribbean pepper sauce
1/2 tsp (2 mL) dried oregano
1/2 tsp (2 mL) paprika
Salt and pepper to taste
Canola oil
1 cup (250 mL) all-purpose flour
Exotic Coleslaw (see recipe, page 120)
1 cup (250 mL) GoomBay Sauce (see recipe, page 5)
1 1/2 cups (375 mL) Guava Bell Pepper Jam (see recipe, page 10)

Harbour Island Lobster Salad in Campari Cups

In The Bahamas, we are known for our rock or spiny tail lobsters that we refer to as crawfish. Unlike Maine Lobsters, The Bahamas crawfish does not have claws but in my opinion the meat is tastier with a more delicate and oceanic flavor.

Serves 6

1. Prepare tomatoes by cutting a thin slice from the top and removing the flesh from the center with a melon baller.
2. In a large bowl, combine lobster meat, onion, jicama, celery, bell pepper, lemon juice, mayonnaise, mustard and oregano and mix well. Add Scotch bonnet pepper (if using) and season with salt and pepper to taste and mix.
3. Spoon 1 Tbsp (15 mL) of the salad into tomatoes to stuff. Garnish with paprika and parsley. To serve, adorn a platter with micro greens around the stuffed tomatoes.

TIP: Campari tomato is the perfect appetizer portion, larger than a cherry tomato, smaller than a plum tomato and noted for its juiciness.

   Did you know that if you simply invert a lobster onto its back for a few minutes, it falls asleep? Some people prefer to do this before placing the lobster in boiling water.

INGREDIENTS

12 Campari tomatoes
2 1/2 lbs (1.1 kg) lobster meat, pre-boiled and shredded
1/2 medium onion, finely diced
1 cup (250 mL) jicama, diced
2 stalks celery, finely diced
1/2 cup (125 mL) orange bell pepper, finely diced
Juice of 3 lemons
2 cups (500 mL) mayonnaise
2 tsp (10 mL) Dijon mustard
1/2 tsp (2 mL) dried oregano
1 Scotch bonnet pepper, finely diced (optional)
Salt and pepper to taste

Garnish

1 tsp (5 mL) smoked paprika
1 Tbsp (15 mL) diced fresh Italian parsley
Micro greens

Grand Bahama Conch Salad

There are many versions of this popular Bahamian dish. Traditionally, it is made simply by using fresh conchs, vegetables, citrus and chili peppers. It's now popular to add a variety of tropical fruits and juices, which is nice if there are more pieces of conch than fruits. I prefer the traditional way with the addition of sweet, crisp and refreshing cucumbers.

Serves 4

1. Place all ingredients in a large bowl and toss. Season to taste with salt and pepper. Divide into bowls (with additional citrus juice), and serve.

   TIP: If fresh conchs are not available, you may try another version by boiling the conchs until tender. The island of Freeport, Grand Bahama, is one of the few islands known for its boiled conch salad. Some islands frown upon it because fresh is best; however, it's still a tasty dish. Follow the recipe, adding 1/4 cup (60 mL) mayonnaise to the boiled version.

INGREDIENTS

4 fresh Queen conchs, diced
1 medium onion, diced
2 ripe tomatoes, diced
1 cucumber, julienned or thinly sliced into 1-inch (2.5 cm) pieces
Juice of 3 limes
Juice of 1 orange
1–2 Scotch bonnet pepper, finely diced
Salt and pepper

Nassau Scorched Conch

The best and only way to eat sweet oceanic scorched conch is fresh out of the shell. Outside of The Bahamas and Caribbean islands, fresh Queen conchs are usually available at Caribbean or Asian live seafood markets. If fresh conchs are not available, substitute with geoduck (a large saltwater clam that is similar in taste.)

Serves 4

1. Fill a large bowl with salt and water and rinse conchs. Transfer to 4 separate serving bowls.
2. Place a few onion rings around each conch. Top with tomatoes and Scotch bonnet pepper.
3. In a small bowl, combine lime and orange juices and pour over conchs.
4. Season with salt and pepper sauce and serve. It is custom to eat the conch by just picking it up by the horn and taking a blissful bite.

TIPS: To score the conch, make diagonal slits with a very sharp knife, turn the conch 90 degrees and make slits to add a crosshatch.

If you're preparing geoduck, parboil the meat first to remove the outer tough skin, then gently pull it away. Score the clam, then follow the recipe.

INGREDIENTS

Salt

4 Queen conchs, scored crosswise (if possible with the horns attached)

1 red onion, thinly sliced into rings

2 ripe tomatoes, chopped

1 Scotch bonnet pepper, finely diced

Juice of 3 limes

Juice of 1 orange

Fine sea salt to taste

2 Tbsp (30 mL) Bahamian Pepper Sauce (see recipe, page 3)

My Bahamian Conch Fritters

Conch fritters are the most requested appetizers throughout
The Bahamas. They're lip-smacking good, and a great starter
for any meal.

Serves 8

1. Put conchs in a large bowl and season with seasoned salt.
   Add onion, celery, green and red bell peppers, fresh and
   ground thyme, flour and baking powder and mix well.
2. Add paste, ketchup, Scotch bonnet pepper, pepper sauce and
   salt and pepper and mix while pouring in the stock to form
   the batter.
3. In a 3-quart (3 L) straight-sided pot, add 3 inches (8 cm) of
   canola oil over medium-high heat. Increase temperature to
   325°F (160°C). (Attach a clip-on frying thermometer to gauge
   heat.)
4. Use a tablespoon or small ice cream scoop to drop batter
   into the oil. The fritters will stick to the bottom of the pot so
   use a slotted spoon to release, allowing fritters to float to the
   top. Turn occasionally with the spoon and let fry until golden
   and cooked inside, about 3–4 minutes.
5. Remove fritters and set aside on a plate lined with paper
   towels.
6. Keep warm and serve immediately with my GoomBay Sauce
   and Green Cocktail Sauce.

INGREDIENTS

2 Queen conchs, tenderized and diced
   (see method, page 18)
3 Tbsp (45 mL) Raquel's Seasoned Salt
   (see recipe, page 2)
1 medium onion, finely diced
1 stalk celery, finely diced
1/4 cup (60 mL) diced green bell pepper
1/4 cup (60 mL) diced red bell pepper
2 tsp (10 mL) fresh thyme leaves
1 tsp (5 mL) ground thyme
4 cups (1 L) all-purpose flour
3 Tbsp (45 mL) baking powder
2 tsp (10 mL) tomato paste
1/2 cup (125 mL) ketchup
1 Scotch bonnet pepper, finely
   diced (optional)
2 Tbsp (30 mL) Caribbean pepper sauce
Salt and pepper to taste
2 cups (500 mL) reserved conch stock
Canola oil
Raquel's GoomBay Sauce (see recipe,
   page 5)
Green Cocktail Sauce (see recipe,
   page 6)

Caribbean Chicken & Veggie Patties with Green Mango Chutney

These island turnovers are blissful bites of exotic spices and flavors. Prepare them in advance and freeze between layers of parchment paper placed in an airtight container. When guests arrive, bake from frozen at 375°F (190°C) until golden, about 25–30 minutes.

Serves 15

1. Preheat oven to 350°F (180°C).
2. To prepare the dough, in a small bowl, combine yeast with warm water and stir until dissolved. Stir in 1 Tbsp (15 mL) of the turmeric.
3. In the bowl of a stand mixer fitted with the paddle attachment, combine flour, remaining turmeric, curry powder and salt and mix.
4. Add the butter and continue mixing. Add egg and gradually add yeast mixture to form the dough. (If the dough is too soft, add a little more flour).
5. Dust a clean surface with flour and knead the dough. Separate into 2 individual balls and let rest for 15 minutes.
6. Using a rolling pin, roll out the first ball of dough evenly to 1/8 inch (3 mm) thick. Line a baking sheet with parchment paper and dust with flour. Use the back of the dough press to cut out circles and set aside on baking sheet.
7. To prepare the chicken filling, in a 4-quart (4 L) pot, heat oil over medium heat. Add onion and sweet potato and cook for 3 minutes. Add ginger, lemongrass and curry powder and cook, stirring, until fragrant, about 2 minutes.
8. Add tomato purée and cook for 3 minutes. Stir in chicken and season with seasoned salt.
9. Add remaining ingredients and cook, stirring occasionally, about 10–15 minutes. Let cool.
10. To prepare the veggie filling, in a 4-quart (4 L) pot, heat oil over medium heat. Add onion, sweet potatoes, curry powder, ginger and lemongrass and cook for 3 minutes. Add tomato purée and cook, stirring occasionally, for 5 minutes more.

INGREDIENTS

Dough

1 miniature dough press
1 Tbsp (15 mL) instant yeast
1 cup (250 mL) warm water
1 1/2 Tbsp (23 mL) ground turmeric, divided
2 1/2 cups (625 mL) all-purpose flour
1 Tbsp (15 mL) Caribbean curry powder
1 tsp (5 mL) salt
1 large egg
3 Tbsp (45 mL) cold butter cubed
Butter or egg wash
1 cup (250 mL) Green Mango Chutney (see recipe, page 6)

Chicken Filling

3 Tbsp (45 mL) olive oil
1 medium onion, diced
1 sweet potato, diced
2 tsp (10 mL) minced ginger
2 tsp (10 mL) lemongrass, finely diced or puréed (outer tough layer removed)
2 Tbsp (30 mL) Caribbean curry powder
1 cup (250 mL) tomato purée
4 skinless chicken thighs, cooked and shredded
1 Tbsp (15 mL) Raquel's Seasoned Salt (see recipe, page 2)
1/2 cup (125 mL) red wine vinegar
1/2 tsp (2 mL) ground thyme
1/2 tsp (2 mL) ground allspice
1 tsp (5 mL) diced fresh basil
1/2 cup (125 mL) coconut milk

11. Add callaloo, cabbage and carrots and cook until the leaves are slightly wilted. Add remaining ingredients and cook, stirring occasionally, for 10 minutes. Let cool.

12. To prepare the patties, center the circle of dough on the bottom of the open dough press, push down on the edges and brush with butter or egg wash to seal.

13. Place 1 tsp (5 mL) of the filling in the center of the dough, close the patty mold and press to seal. Remove the sealed patty from the mold and set aside on the baking sheet. Repeat forming the remaining dough into patties, then brush patties lightly with egg wash. Bake for 15–20 minutes. Serve with Green Mango Chutney.

1 Scotch bonnet pepper, finely diced
1 Tbsp (15 mL) peanut sauce (optional)
Salt and pepper to taste
1 Tbsp (15 mL) diced fresh
   Italian parsley

Veggie Filling
3 Tbsp (45 mL) olive oil
1/2 medium onion, diced
2 sweet potatoes, diced
1 Tbsp (15 mL) Caribbean curry powder
1 tsp (5 mL) minced ginger
1 tsp (5 mL) finely diced or puréed
   lemongrass
1 cup (250 mL) tomato purée
2 cups (500 mL) shredded callaloo
   leaves
1/2 cup (125 mL) shredded red cabbage
1/2 cup (125 mL) coarsely grated carrots
1/2 cup (125 mL) coconut milk
1 tsp (5 mL) dried Italian seasoning
1 tsp (5 mL) fresh basil leaves
1/4 cup (60 mL) fresh chadon beni or
   cilantro (see page 222)
1/4 tsp (1 mL) ground thyme
1/4 tsp (1 mL) ground allspice
1 Scotch bonnet pepper, finely diced
1 Tbsp (15 mL) peanut sauce
Salt and pepper to taste

Creamy Rock Lobster Mac 'n' Cheese

Serve this dish in ovenproof crock bowls and make a grand entrance to the dining table with a platter of the most enticing, sizzling-cheese sauce, oozing around morsels of sweet-succulent lobster meat.

Serves 6

1. Preheat oven to 375°F (190°C).
2. In a large bowl, toss together lobster meat, seafood seasoning and lemon juice.
3. In a large skillet, heat oil over medium heat. Par-cook lobster for 3–5 minutes. Set aside in a small dish.
4. Fill a 4-quart (4 L) pot halfway with water and bring to a boil over medium-high heat.
5. Add onion, celery, bell pepper and pasta and cook until aldente, about 8–10 minutes. Drain in a colander and transfer to a large bowl.
6. Add butter and 2 cups (500 mL) of the white cheddar to the bowl and mix to melt.
7. Add evaporated milk and 2 cups (500 mL) of the cream and mix. Add eggs and mix well.
8. Add remaining cheddar, Parmigiano-Reggiano and season to taste with salt and pepper. Add sour cream and mix well.
9. Divide pasta into ovenproof bowls or ramekins. Place a few pieces of lobster meat over pasta and then cover with Gruyère cheese. Bake for about 20 minutes or until cheese is melted and oozing. Drizzle with curry oil and serve at once with crusty toasted baguettes.

INGREDIENTS

1 lb (450 g) lobster meat, cut into 1-inch (2.5 cm) pieces
1 Tbsp (15 mL) seafood seasoning
Juice of 1/2 lemon
1/4 cup (60 mL) olive oil
1 sweet onion, finely diced
2 stalks celery, finely diced
1/2 yellow bell pepper, diced
3 cups (750 mL) elbow pasta
1/4 cup (60 mL) butter, cut into cubes
4 cups (1 L) grated white cheddar cheese, divided
2 cups (500 mL) evaporated milk
4 cups (1 L) whipping (or heavy) cream (35%), divided
2 whole eggs, slightly beaten
1 1/2 cups (375 mL) grated Parmigiano-Reggiano
1 1/2 cups (375 mL) sour cream
2 cups (500 mL) grated Gruyère cheese
Salt and white pepper to taste
1/2 cup (125 mL) Curry Oil (see recipe, page 7)
Crusty toasted baguettes

COD FISH FRITTERS

I grew up eating these tasty spicy fritters that originate from Jamaica. Saltfish is cod that has been preserved by drying after salting. It should be soaked overnight in water to eliminate most of the salt.

Serves 8

1. Soak saltfish for 1 hour (or overnight) in a medium bowl. Remove and transfer to a 3-quart (3 L) pot filled halfway with water.

2. Place pot over medium-high heat and bring to a boil. Reduce heat and simmer, about 10–15 minutes. Reserve water and separate the codfish for the batter. Set aside.

3. In a large skillet, melt butter over medium heat. Add onion and sweat for 3 minutes. Add garlic and cook for 1 minute.

4. Add green and red bell pepper and tomato purée and cook for 3 minutes. Remove from heat and set aside.

5. In a large bowl, combine remaining ingredients (except canola oil) and mix, gradually adding the reserved liquid to make the batter. Adjust seasoning.

6. In a 3-quart (3 L) straight-sided pot, add 3 inches (8 cm) canola oil and heat over medium-high heat. Bring temperature to 325°F (160°C). (Attach a clip-on frying thermometer to gauge heat.)

7. Use a tablespoon or small ice cream scoop to drop the batter into the oil. The fritter will stick to the bottom of the pot so use a slotted spoon to release it, allowing the fritter to float to the top. Turn occasionally with the spoon and let fry until golden and cooked inside, about 4 minutes.

8. Remove fritters and set aside on a plate lined with paper towels.

TIP: Serve accompanied with Island Currant Ketchup (see recipe, page 8) or Lemongrass & Dill Dipping Sauce (see recipe, page 7).

INGREDIENTS

1/2 lb (225 g) boneless saltfish

3 Tbsp (45 mL) unsalted butter

1/2 medium onion, diced

4 cloves garlic, diced

1/4 piece green bell pepper, finely diced

1/4 piece red bell pepper, finely diced

1/2 cup (125 mL) tomato purée

4 cups (1 L) all-purpose flour

3 Tbsp (45 mL) baking powder

1 Tbsp (15 mL) light brown sugar

1/2 Tbsp (7.5 mL) Raquel's Seasoned Salt (see recipe, page 2)

3 sprigs fresh thyme, stripped from stem

2 Tbsp (30 mL) Maggi Seasoning

2 cups (500 mL) reserved liquid

Salt and pepper to taste

1 1/2 Scotch bonnet peppers, finely diced

Canola or vegetable oil

Savory Lamb Turnovers

It is a pet peeve of mine to attend a special event when during the first cocktail hour the servers parade around with miniscule, unappetizing starters or amuse-bouche. Why save the best for last? Extraordinary appetizers always set the tone for the evening! These lamb turnovers are "dressed to impress" and simply unforgettable.

Serves 20

1. Preheat oven to 350°F (180°C).
2. To prepare the dough, in a small bowl, combine yeast with warm water and stir until dissolved.
3. In bowl of a stand mixer fitted with paddle attachment, combine flour, salt, sugar, basil and chives and mix.
4. Add egg and olive oil and gradually add yeast mixture to form the dough (if the dough is too soft, add a little more flour).
5. Dust a clean surface with flour and knead the dough. Separate into 2 individual balls and let rest for 15 minutes.
6. Using a rolling pin, roll out the first ball of dough evenly to 1/8 inch (3 mm) thick. Line a baking sheet with parchment paper and dust with flour. Use the back of the dough press to cut out circles and set aside on baking sheet.
7. In a large skillet, heat oil over medium heat. Add ground lamb and cook, while breaking up the pieces with a wooden spoon, about 5–10 minutes. Season with salt and garlic powder.
8. Add onion and cook for 3 minutes. Add minced garlic, bell pepper, chadon beni and ginger and cook, stirring occasionally, for 3 minutes. Drain and transfer to a large bowl.
9. Add rosemary, cinnamon, Italian seasoning, ketchup and salt

continued on next page

INGREDIENTS

Dough
1 miniature dough press
2 Tbsp (30 mL) instant yeast
2 cups (500 mL) warm water
4 cups (1 L) all-purpose flour
1 tsp (5 mL) salt
3 Tbsp (45 mL) granulated sugar
3 Tbsp (45 mL) minced fresh basil
2 Tbsp (30 mL) minced fresh chives
1 large egg
1/4 cup (60 mL) olive oil

3 Tbsp (45 mL) olive oil
2 lbs (1 kg) ground lamb
1 tsp (5 mL) salt
1 tsp (5 mL) garlic powder
1 medium onion, diced
4 cloves garlic, minced
1/2 red bell pepper, diced
1/4 cup (60 mL) diced chadon beni or
    fresh Italian parsley
1 cup (250 mL) diced candied ginger
1 Tbsp (15 mL) ground rosemary
1 tsp (5 mL) ground cinnamon
1 Tbsp (15 mL) Italian seasoning
1 cup (250 mL) ketchup
1/2 cup (125 mL) plain bread crumbs
Salt and pepper to taste
Butter or egg wash
1 cup (250 mL) Mint Crème (see recipe,
    page 4)
1 cup (250 mL) pine nuts, toasted

and pepper to taste and mix well.

10. To prepare the turnovers, center the circle of dough on the bottom of the open dough press, push down on the edges and brush with butter or egg wash to seal.

11. Place 1 tsp (5 mL) of the filling in the center of the dough, close the mold and press to seal. Remove the turnover from the press and set aside on the baking sheet. Repeat forming the remaining dough into turnovers, then brush patties lightly with egg wash. Bake in the oven, about 15–20 minutes. Let cool.

12. Fill a piping bag with Mint Crème and dot generously on top of each turnover. Top with a few pine nuts and serve.

TROPICAL FRUIT CHEESE LOG

This cheese log is a perfect accompaniment to any charcuterie plate. Exotic fruits, herbs and spices are blended with soft unripened goat cheese.

Serves 12

1. In a large bowl, stir all ingredients together (except for nuts and pita) and mix well. Transfer to a plate.
2. Spread pistachios on a plate and set aside.
3. Divide mixture into two 8- to 10-inch (20–25 cm) logs. Roll logs in pistachios to coat. Sprinkle water on 2 pieces of plastic wrap and transfer each cheese log onto the wraps. Roll to cover and seal the edges by twisting and folding under the log. Refrigerate for 2 hours or overnight. Serve accompanied with toasted pita wedges or vegetable sticks.

TIP: Canned guavas are readily available at Caribbean and Latin Supermarkets.

INGREDIENTS

2 cups (500 mL) soft unripened goat cheese, at room temperature
2 cups (500 mL) cream cheese, softened
1 tsp (5 mL) roasted garlic purée
Zest of 1 lemon
2 Tbsp (30 mL) finely diced red bell pepper
1 Tbsp (15 mL) finely grated carrot
2 pink canned guava shells, diced
2 dried mango slices or mamey, diced
1 dried pineapple slice, diced
2 fresh basil leaves, diced
1 Tbsp (15 mL) diced fresh Italian parsley
1/2 cup (125 mL) pistachios, coarsely chopped
Toasted pita wedges or vegetable sticks

Pear-a-dise Thin Crust Pizza with Smoked Duck & Goat Cheese Crumble

Our restaurant's specialty was exceptional thin crust pizzas with unique toppings gathered from my travels throughout Europe and North America. The thin crust pizzas at The Wine Lounge gained recognition when *USA Today* voted our restaurant one of the 10 best lounges in the Bahamas. Pear-a-dise pizza is inspired by my love for the diversity of fresh and sustainable ingredients. Cheers to exceptional cuisines!

Makes two 10-inch (25 cm) pizzas

1. Preheat oven to 500°F (260°C).
2. To prepare the pizza dough, in a small bowl, combine yeast with warm water and stir until dissolved.
3. In the bowl of a stand mixer fitted with the paddle attachment, add flour and salt. Add egg and olive oil and mix. Gradually add the yeast mixture to form the dough (if the dough is too soft, add a little more flour).
4. Dust a clean surface with flour and knead the dough, separate into 2 individual balls and let rest for 15 minutes.
5. Dust the surface with flour again. Using a rolling pin, roll out the first ball of dough evenly 1/4-inch (6 mm) thick for a thin crust pizza.
6. Pierce the dough with a fork or a pastry docker to promote even baking. Set the dough aside on a 12-inch (30 cm) pizza pan sprayed with oil.
7. To prepare the glazed pears, in a 2-quart (2 L) saucepan, combine Marsala wine and sugar over medium heat and stir to dissolve. Remove pan from heat and add sliced pears to steep.

continued on next page 106

INGREDIENTS

Pizza Dough
1 Tbsp (15 mL) instant yeast
1 cup (250 mL) warm water
2 1/2 cups (625 mL) all-purpose flour
1 tsp (5 mL) salt
1 large egg
3 Tbsp (45 mL) olive oil

Glazed Pears
2 cups (500 mL) Marsala wine
1/2 cup (125 mL) granulated sugar
1 Bosch pear, sliced into
   1/4-inch (6 mm) pieces

Coconut-Curry Sauce
2 Tbsp (30 mL) olive oil
1 Tbsp (15 mL) Caribbean curry powder
1/2 tsp (2 mL) ground turmeric
1/2 tsp (2 mL) ground cumin
1/2 tsp (2 mL) ground ginger
1/4 tsp (1 mL) ground thyme
2 cups (500 mL) coconut cream
1 Tbsp (15 mL) light brown sugar
Salt and white pepper to taste
continued on next page 106

8. To prepare the coconut-curry sauce, in a small saucepan, heat oil over medium heat. Add curry powder, turmeric, cumin, ginger and thyme and cook until the oils are released and fragrant, about 3 minutes. Stir in coconut cream and sugar. Reduce heat and simmer until sauce is slightly thickened to coat the back of a spoon. Adjust seasoning with salt and pepper.

9. Spread 3 Tbsp (45 mL) of the tomato sauce over each pizza dough and add half of the mozzarella cheese, then add onion slices around the pies.

10. Transfer pizzas to the preheated oven. Bake for 3–4 minutes for cracker thin pizza pies.

11. To assemble the pizzas, add pear slices, duck meat, arugula and goat cheese.

12. Pour curry sauce into dipping cups, add a few drops of the vinaigrette and make a pattern by pulling lines or swirling the sauce around with a toothpick for an appealing presentation.

13. Slice pie evenly with a pastry cutter and serve with the sauce to drizzle over the pizza.

TIPS: Pears are more flavorful if steeped overnight in the refrigerator in an airtight container but can be used right away in this recipe, if desired.

If you don't have a pizza stone, bake the pies inside 2 nonstick 10-inch (25 cm) perforated pizza pans. Assemble the pies on the pans, then place in the oven at 500°F (260°C) and bake for 3 minutes.

6 Tbsp (90 mL) Homemade Tomato Sauce (see recipe, page 8)
3 cups (750 mL) shredded mozzarella cheese, divided
1/2 cup (125 mL) sliced red onion
1 smoked duck breast, thinly sliced
1 cup (250 mL) rocket arugula
1/2 cup (125 mL) crumbled goat cheese
1/2 cup (125 mL) Green Vinaigrette, strained (see recipe, page 4)

Abaco Stone Crabs with Lemongrass & Dill Dipping Sauce

Entice your guests with a centerpiece of these sustainable and mouthwatering crab claws. Display them piled high over crushed ice with lemon wedges and a bright and citrusy dipping sauce.

Serves 10

1. Stone crabs are sold pre-cooked. Fill a large bowl with cold salted water, add claws and rinse in the water.
2. Place each claw in a towel (to prevent the shell from splattering), then lightly crack the knuckle on both sides with a mallet.
3. Serve chilled over a platter or large serving bowl with crushed ice, lemon wedges and Lemongrass & Dill Dipping Sauce.

INGREDIENTS

Salt
15 lbs (6.8 kg) stone crab claws
2 cups (500 mL) Lemongrass & Dill
  Dipping Sauce (see recipe, page 7)
Crushed ice
Lemon wedges

Curry Chicken Pizza

If you're wondering what to do with a leftover curry dish, transform it into a delectable thin crust pizza.

Makes two 10-inch (25 cm) pizzas

1. Preheat oven to 500°F (260°C).
2. Set prepared dough aside on two 12-inch (30 cm) pizza pans sprayed with oil.
3. Spread 3 Tbsp (45 mL) of the tomato sauce over pizza dough and half the mozzarella cheese. Arrange half of the curry chicken and potatoes over the pizza. Repeat with the other dough, using remaining tomato sauce, mozzarella cheese and curry chicken.
4. Transfer pizzas to the preheated oven on the center and top racks. Bake for about 3–4 minutes for cracker thin pizza pies.
5. In a small dish, mix cumin, cardamom and fennel together and set aside.
6. To assemble the pizzas, drizzle with curry oil, if using. Garnish with green onions and the spice mixture. Cut and serve at once.

INGREDIENTS

Pizza Dough (see recipe, page 104)
6 Tbsp (90 mL) Homemade Tomato Sauce (see recipe, page 8), divided
3 cups (750 mL) shredded mozzarella cheese, divided
2 cups (500 mL) Island Curry Chicken with Sweet Potatoes, chicken shredded (see recipe, page 143), divided
1 tsp (5 mL) ground cumin
1 tsp (5 mL) ground cardamom
1/2 tsp (2 mL) ground fennel

Garnish

Curry Oil (see recipe, page 7) (optional)
1/2 cup (125 mL) green onions, thinly sliced on the diagonal

Twice-Fried Plantains with Caribbean Mango Salsa

This popular sweet, salty and crispy appetizer or side dish is relished throughout the Caribbean. It's known as tostones in Latin American countries, where it's served along with salsa as an appetizer.
Serves 6

1. Preheat a deep fryer with oil to 350°F (180°C).
2. In a medium bowl, add water and 1 Tbsp (15 mL) of the salt and stir to dissolve.
3. Peel plantains and reserve the skin. Cut plantains on the diagonal into 1-inch (2.5 cm) slices. Transfer plantains to the basket of the deep fryer and fry until golden. Using tongs, transfer plantains to the bowl of salted water and soak for 3 minutes.
4. To flatten the plantains—if you don't have a plantain press (tostenera)—use the reserved outer skin to flatten the tropical fruit one at a time into 1/4-inch (6 mm) thick slices. Set aside on a plate lined with paper towels to dry while repeating with the other pieces.
5. Return plantains to the deep-fryer basket and fry again until crispy, about 2–3 minutes more. Transfer to another plate lined with paper towels and sprinkle immediately with remaining salt. Serve topped with Caribbean Mango Salsa and garnish with cilantro.

TIP: For an alternative treat, try these plantains topped with my Guava Bell Pepper Jam (see recipe, page 10).

INGREDIENTS

Canola or vegetable oil
4 cups (1 L) of water
2 Tbsp (30 mL) sea salt divided
2 yellow half-ripe plantains
Caribbean Mango Salsa (see recipe, page 9)
Cilantro, for garnish

Island Crab Cakes Wrapped in Seaweed

Patrons of my restaurant, couldn't get enough of these delectable crab cakes wrapped with ribbons of nori (Asian seaweed) that complemented the cakes with a smoky-briny flavor
 . . . pure bliss!

Serves 4

1. Preheat a deep fryer with oil to 350°F (180°C).
2. In a medium bowl, combine all ingredients (except nori and flour) and mix thoroughly.
3. Wrap 2 ribbons of nori crosswise around the cakes (to resemble a parcel), cut off the extra length and set cakes aside on a plate lined with parchment.
4. Lightly dust cakes with flour, then transfer to the basket of the deep fryer and fry until golden on both sides. Transfer to another plate lined with paper towels.

TIP: Serve crab cakes accompanied with Tamarind Glaze and Grilling Sauce (see recipe, page 12) or Sweet Peppery Tartar Sauce (see recipe, page 5).

INGREDIENTS

Canola or vegetable oil
2 cups (500 mL) lump crabmeat
1/2 cup (125 mL) mayonnaise
1 tsp (5 mL) Dijon mustard
Juice of 1 lime
1/2 tsp (2 mL) cayenne pepper
2 Tbsp (30 mL) panko bread crumbs
2 green onions, thinly sliced on
  the diagonal
2 cloves garlic, diced
1 chadon beni leaf diced (optional)
1/4 cup (60 mL) diced red bell pepper
1/4 tsp (2 mL) smoked paprika
Salt and pepper to taste
2 sheets nori (dried seaweed), cut into
  1/4-inch (6 mm) strips
1/2 cup (125 mL) all-purpose flour
  for dusting

TROPICAL MANGO SHRIMP ON LEMONGRASS SKEWERS

Enjoy the rich taste of these wild prawns vibrantly flavored with a citrusy glaze.

Serves 6

1. Lightly season prawns with seafood seasoning and set aside in a medium bowl.
2. In a 2-quart (2 L) saucepan, combine mango juice concentrate, butter, lemon, sugar, cinnamon, lemongrass powder and paprika over medium heat and bring to a boil. Reduce heat and simmer for 15 minutes or until sauce thickens enough to coat the back of a spoon. Let cool.
3. Pour half of the sauce over the prawns, cover with plastic wrap and transfer to the refrigerator to marinate for 1 hour (could be done a day in advance). Reserve remaining sauce for basting.
4. Preheat barbecue grill. Remove the tough outer layers from lemongrass stalks and discard. Beat stalks a few times with a mallet to release their fragrant oils.
5. Toss lemongrass stalks with oil. Grill for about 1 minute on each side for grill marks to appear. Set aside on a plate and let cool.
6. Thread 3–4 shrimps onto each stalk and grill while basting on both sides with reserved sauce until opaque, about 2–3 minutes per side. Transfer to a platter and garnish with coconut and cilantro and serve at once.

INGREDIENTS

1 lb (450 g) large prawns, peeled and deveined
1/4 cup (60 mL) seafood seasoning
1 cup (250 mL) frozen mango juice concentrate
2 Tbsp (30 mL) butter
Juice of 1/2 lemon
1/2 cup (125 mL) coconut palm sugar
1 tsp (5 mL) ground cinnamon
1/2 tsp (2 mL) lemongrass powder or paste
1/2 tsp (2 mL) smoked paprika
6 lemongrass stalks
3 Tbsp (45 mL) vegetable oil

Garnish
1/4 cup (60 mL) toasted coconut flakes
1/4 cup (60 mL) cilantro or parsley leaves, diced

Bimini Coconut Cracked Lobster

This dish is simply delightful. Sweet succulent morsels of lobster are dipped in a coconut-buttermilk batter, then deep fried until golden and complemented with three island dipping sauces.
Serves 6

1. Fill a deep fryer with oil and preheat to 350°F (180°F).
2. In a medium bowl, place lobster meat and season with seafood seasoning. Set aside.
3. To prepare the wet batter, in a medium bowl, combine buttermilk and coconut milk powder. Whisk in eggs, flour and salt. Set aside.
4. To prepare the dry batter, place the coconut on a plate and remaining flour on another. Add black pepper to the flour mixture and mix with a fork. Set aside to line up a dredging station.
5. To assemble, place lobster pieces into the wet batter. Remove with a slotted spoon and transfer to the plate with flour; coat, dip into the wet batter again then transfer to plate with coconut and roll to coat again. Transfer lobster to the basket of the deep fryer and fry until golden. Serve accompanied with dipping sauces and lemon wedges.

INGREDIENTS

Canola or vegetable oil
2 lbs (1 kg) lobster meat, cut into
 1-inch (2.5 cm) pieces
1/4 cup (60 mL) seafood seasoning
2 cups (500 mL) buttermilk
1 cup (250 mL) coconut milk powder
2 large eggs, lightly beaten
2 1/4 cups (540 mL) all-purpose flour
1/2 tsp (2 mL) salt
2 cups (500 mL) unsweetened
 coconut flakes
2 cups (500 mL) all-purpose flour
1 tsp (5 mL) freshly ground black pepper
2 cups (500 mL) Sweet Peppery Tartar
 Sauce (see recipe, page 5)
2 cups (500 mL) Green Cocktail Sauce
 (see recipe, page 6)
2 cups (500 mL) Guava Bell Pepper Jam
 (see recipe, page 10)
Lemon wedges, for garnish

STEAMED HAMBURGER SLIDERS WITH
ISLAND CURRANT KETCHUP

If you've never had a luscious steamed hamburger, you're missing out! These old-fashioned hamburgers are legendary. They are seasoned with earthy spices, fresh herbs and vegetables, then steamed with beer to perfection. Serve with Exotic Chips (see recipe, page 16).

Serves 8

1. Preheat the oven broiler on high heat.
2. In a large skillet, cook bacon over medium heat until crispy. Set aside on a plate lined with paper towels.
3. In a large bowl, combine beef, pork, onion, garlic, bell pepper, jalapeño, seasoned salt, cumin, thyme and parsley and mix thoroughly with your hands.
4. Add egg and bread crumbs and continue to mix well. Line a baking sheet with parchment paper.
5. Using 1/4 cup (60 mL) at a time, portion out meat and form into 8 miniature hamburgers while shaping with your hands. Set aside on the prepared sheet.
6. To steam the hamburgers, place a steam basket over a 4-quart (4 L) pot with 2–3 inches (5–8 cm) of beer. Add 2–3 of the hamburgers, spacing them each 1 inch (2.5 cm) apart. Turn heat to high and bring beer to a boil. Reduce heat to steam and cover with a lid that's slightly ajar allowing the steam to escape.
7. Steam hamburgers for 5 minutes or test with a thermometer to reach an internal temperature of 160°F (71°C). Carefully remove hamburgers with a spatula or tongs and transfer to another baking sheet lined with parchment. Top 4 burgers with 1 slice of white cheddar each and the other 4 burgers

continued on next page

INGREDIENTS

16 slices apple wood smoked bacon, divided

2 lbs (1 kg) ground beef

1/2 lb (225 g) ground pork

1/2 large sweet onion, finely diced

6 cloves garlic, finely diced

1/2 red bell pepper, finely diced

1 jalapeño, finely diced

2 Tbsp (30 mL) Raquel's Seasoned Salt (see recipe, page 2)

1 tsp (5 mL) ground cumin

1 tsp (5 mL) ground thyme

1/4 cup (60 mL) diced fresh Italian parsley

1 large egg

1 cup (250 mL) plain bread crumbs

2 cups (500 mL) lager or ale beer

4 slices white cheddar cheese

4 slices yellow cheddar cheese

16 slider buns or sweet rolls, lightly toasted

1 1/2 cups (375 mL) GoomBay Sauce (see recipe, page 5)

2 cups (500 mL) spring lettuce mix

4 plum tomatoes, sliced

1 small red onion, thinly sliced

16 slices pickles

2 cups (500 mL) Island Currant Ketchup (see recipe, page 8)

with yellow cheddar. Transfer burgers to the preheated broiler to melt the cheese for 1 minute. Repeat with remaining hamburgers.

8. To assemble the sliders, place buns on a platter and generously spread GoomBay Sauce over them. Top with lettuce, patties, bacon, tomatoes, onion, pickles and Island Currant Ketchup. Repeat with remaining burgers and serve with fries and a side of Island Currant Ketchup.

TIP: To refrigerate or freeze uncooked hamburgers, place patties on wax paper, then top with another piece of wax paper and store in resealable freezer bags or in an airtight container. Meat should always be placed at the bottom of your refrigerator in a separate compartment. Refrigerate hamburgers for a maximum of 2 days.

Tamarind Chickpea Dip with Mamey Crema

An opulent vegetarian dish complimented with a native fruit…
"fit for a king!"

Serves 8

1. To prepare the mamey crema, in a small bowl, place sour cream. Add lemon juice and fold in mamey purée. Cover with plastic wrap and refrigerate.
2. Rinse chickpeas in a colander under cold running water. Drain and set aside.
3. In a large skillet, heat ghee over medium heat. Add curry powder, cumin, onion and garlic and cook, stirring occasionally, for 2 minutes.
4. Add tomatoes, chadon beni and potato and cook for 2 minutes more.
5. Add ketchup and water and bring to a boil while stirring. Add chickpeas. Reduce heat and simmer and continue to cook, about 15 minutes.
6. Add Scotch bonnet pepper (if using) and season to taste with salt and pepper.
7. To assemble the dip, in a 3-quart (3 L) glass or trifle bowl, place chickpeas. Spread tamarind chutney over chickpeas, then layer with mamey crema. Garnish with chives and mustard seeds. Serve with toasted pita or naan wedges.

INGREDIENTS

Mamey Crema
3 cups (750 mL) sour cream
1 tsp (5 mL) lemon juice
1/2 cup (125 mL) mamey pulp, puréed

4 cups (1 L) canned chickpeas
3 Tbsp (45 mL) ghee
1/4 cup (60 mL) Caribbean curry powder
1 tsp (5 mL) ground cumin
1/2 medium onion, diced
4 cloves garlic, diced
2 cups (500 mL) diced tomatoes
3 chadon beni leaves, chiffonade
1 large Caribbean sweet potato, diced
1/4 cup (60 mL) ketchup
2 cups (500 mL) water
1 Scotch bonnet pepper, finely diced (optional)
Salt and pepper to taste
3 cups (750 mL) Tamarind Chutney (see recipe, page 9)

Garnish
1 Tbsp (15 mL) chives, diced
1 Tbsp (15 mL) black mustard seeds, toasted
Toasted pita, or naan wedges, for serving

GREAT INAGUA CRAB SALAD MELTS

The island of Inagua is the southernmost district of The Bahamas, consisting of Great Inagua and Little Inagua. It's also known for its wonderfully strange-looking black land crabs. Enjoy this delectable salad over fresh toasted baguettes.

Serves 8

1. Preheat the oven broiler on high.
2. In a large bowl, combine all ingredients for the crab salad and mix well.
3. Line a baking sheet with parchment paper. Drizzle baguette slices with oil then place on baking sheet and spread crab salad over top. Sprinkle generously with cheese and top with tomatoes. Transfer to the preheated oven for about 1–2 minutes or until cheese melts.
4. Remove melts from the oven. Place on a platter and garnish with fresh oregano leaves; serve immediately.

INGREDIENTS

Crab Salad
4 cups (1 L) lump blue crabmeat
1/2 onion, finely diced
1 stalk celery, finely diced
1/4 cup (60 mL) finely diced red
 bell pepper
1/2 Scotch bonnet pepper, finely diced
Juice of 2 limes
2 cups (500 mL) mayonnaise
1 tsp (5 mL) Dijon mustard
1 Tbsp (15 mL) Raquel's Seasoned Salt
 (see recipe, page 2)

1 loaf French baguette, slices toasted
1/4 cup (60 mL) olive oil
1 cup (250 mL) grated Gruyère cheese
1 cup (250 mL) heirloom cherry
 tomatoes, cut in half
1/4 cup (60 mL) fresh oregano leaves,
 for garnish

DINING IN PARADISE   119   BREEZY ISLAND STARTERS & SALADS

Exotic Coleslaw

Here's a taste of paradise with fresh, bright citrusy flavors. Serve in a hollow pineapple shell for an extremely appetizing display.
Serves 8

1. In a large bowl, combine ingredients and mix thoroughly. Adjust seasoning and serve in a hollow pineapple shell.

INGREDIENTS

1/2 head green cabbage, thinly shredded
1/4 head red cabbage, thinly shredded
1 carrot, grated
3 green onions, thinly sliced on
  the diagonal
1/2 cup (125 mL) coconut flakes
1/2 cup (125 mL) golden raisins
1/4 cup (60 mL) crushed pineapple
2 cups (500 mL) mayonnaise
2 tsp (10 mL) Dijon mustard
1 Tbsp (15 mL) granulated sugar
1 cup (250 mL) coconut water
1 cup (250 mL) pineapple juice or soda
Salt and pepper to taste
1 pineapple shell, hollowed, for serving

LADY PAT'S AWARD-WINNING POTATO SALAD

Pat's traditional Sunday brunches are "the talk of the town." When it comes to scrumptious Bahamian cuisine, she can throw down with the best of them. I was fortunate to inherit the recipe for her sensational potato salad, as it's still the best I've ever tasted.

Serves 6

1. In a 4-quart (4 L) pot, place potatoes and eggs over medium-high heat. Add salted water to cover. Bring to a boil.
2. Cook until potatoes are tender when pierced with a knife. Remove potatoes and let cool. Cut into wedges. Cut each wedge into 1/2-inch (1 cm) pieces on the diagonal and set aside on a baking sheet lined with paper towels.
3. Transfer potatoes to a large bowl. Shell boiled eggs and slice thinly.
4. Divide egg slices into 2 portions. Set aside half for garnishing and cut the other half into 1/4-inch (6 mm) pieces. Add to the bowl with the potatoes.
5. Add remaining ingredients (except for parsley and paprika) and mix while mashing one quarter of the potatoes. Adjust seasoning and garnish with remaining egg slices, parsley and paprika. Serve at once.

INGREDIENTS

4 russet potatoes, peeled
4 large eggs
1 Tbsp (15 mL) salt
1/2 medium onion, finely diced
1/4 cup (60 mL) finely diced green bell pepper
1/2 Scotch bonnet pepper, finely diced
1 1/2 cups (375 mL) mayonnaise
1 Tbsp (15 mL) Dijon mustard
Salt to taste
1 Tbsp (15 mL) finely diced fresh Italian parsley
1/4 tsp (2 mL) smoked paprika, for garnish

NATIVE CORN & CHARRED PEPPER SALAD

Flavorful bell peppers impart an earthy flavor to this subtle-sweet and fresh corn salad that is a tasty accompaniment to barbecues or roasts.

Serves 6

1. Preheat oven to 400°F (200°C)
2. To prepare the vinaigrette, in the bowl of a food processor, combine mustard, vinegar and cumin. With the motor running, gradually pour in oil. Adjust seasoning with salt and pepper, and set aside.
3. Line a baking sheet with parchment paper. Place poblano and red and orange bell peppers on the sheet and drizzle with oil.
4. Roast peppers in the oven until skins are charred, turning occasionally, for 30 minutes. Transfer peppers to a bowl and cover with plastic wrap for 5 minutes. Peel off skins and discard. Dice peppers and set aside.
5. In a small skillet, toast fennel seeds over low heat for 2 minutes or until fragrant. Let cool. Transfer to a spice grinder and grind seeds. Set aside.
6. Follow package instructions to cook quinoa. Let cool and transfer to a large bowl.
7. Remove kernels from corn with a knife and add to the bowl with quinoa.
8. Add roasted peppers, fennel, shallots, tomatoes, cilantro and vinaigrette and toss. Garnish with cheese and serve in lettuce cups.

TIP: An alternative way of charring peppers is by placing them directly over a gas burner on medium-high heat. As the skin turns black, rotate peppers with tongs until all sides are charred. Transfer peppers to a medium stainless-steel bowl and cover with plastic wrap for 5 minutes. Remove wrap and peel off charred skins and dice.

INGREDIENTS

Vinaigrette
1 Tbsp (15 mL) Dijon mustard
1/4 cup (60 mL) champagne or white wine vinegar
1/4 tsp (1 mL) ground cumin
1/2 cup (125 mL) extra virgin olive oil
Salt and pepper to taste

1 poblano pepper
1 red bell pepper
1 orange bell pepper
3 Tbsp (45 mL) olive oil
1 tsp (5 mL) fennel seeds
2 cups (500 mL) quinoa
3 ears corn, husked and cooked
2 shallots, diced
2 cups (500 mL) cherry tomatoes, halved
1/4 cup (60 mL) diced cilantro leaves
1/2 cup (125 mL) crumbled goat cheese
1 head butter lettuce

Vangie's Broccoflower Salad

My mother-in-law was a very talented cook who inspired me to always do my best. I enjoyed watching her cook an elegant meal; it was as if I were watching a performance of Swan Lake at the theater. She was so incredibly graceful in the kitchen. Broccoflower is slightly sweeter than broccoli, which makes this festive salad simply delightful. Take it with you to a potluck dinner and make friends with this conversation starter.

Serves 10

1. Position oven rack on top and preheat to 350°F (180°C). Line 2 baking sheets with parchment paper and set aside.
2. Place broccoflower and cauliflower on the baking sheets. Sprinkle with salt and pepper and drizzle with half of the olive oil. Bake on the top of the preheated oven, about 25 minutes.
3. In a small bowl, combine cumin, coriander and cinnamon. In a medium bowl, add carrots and toss with remaining oil, spice mix, salt and pepper and place on the other baking sheet. Bake for about 30–35 minutes. Let cool for 5 minutes.
4. Meanwhile, in a small bowl, combine mayonnaise, honey and Parmigiano-Reggiano and mix thoroughly. Cover with plastic wrap and set aside in the refrigerator.
5. In a 2-quart (2 L) saucepan, combine vinegar and brown sugar and dissolve over medium heat. Add onion and cook for 5 minutes. Remove from heat and let steep.
6. In a large bowl, combine broccoflower, cauliflower, carrots and onions and toss with honey-mayo dressing. Garnish with crumble, pine nuts and lemon zest.

TIP: As another option, you could blanche the Romanesco and cauliflower for a vibrant presentation.

INGREDIENTS

1 head broccoflower (florets separated) or 8 Romanesco broccoli,
2 cups (500 mL) white or cheddar cauliflower florets
2 cups (500 mL) florets purple cauliflower (optional)
Salt and pepper to taste
1 cup (250 mL) olive oil, divided
2 tsp (10 mL) ground cumin
1/2 tsp (2 mL) ground coriander
1/2 tsp (2 mL) ground cinnamon
2 cups (500 mL) baby carrots
4 cups (1 L) mayonnaise
1/4 cup (60 mL) honey
1/2 cup (125 mL) grated Parmigiano-Reggiano
1 medium red onion, thinly sliced
1 cup (250 mL) apple cider vinegar
1 tsp (5 mL) brown sugar
1 cup (250 mL) Johnny Cake Crumble (see Variation, page 13)
1/2 cup (125 mL) pine nuts, toasted
Zest of 2 lemons

Vangie's Delicious Layered Salad

This salad of multiple layers of crisp green vegetables is marinated overnight in a rich and creamy dressing with citrus nuances.

Serves 8

1. In a small bowl, combine ingredients for dressing and mix well. Set aside.
2. Separate lettuce leaves and layer half to cover the bottom of a 13- x 9-inch (33 x 23 cm) baking dish.
3. Layer half of the onion, peas and cucumber over the lettuce. Follow with half of the dressing, then layer with slices of eggs and repeat.
4. Garnish with cheese and parsley. Cover with plastic wrap and refrigerate overnight for the flavors to set.

INGREDIENTS

Citrus Dressing

2 cups (500 mL) mayonnaise

1/4 cup (60 mL) half-and-half cream (10%)

1 tsp (5 mL) orange zest

1 tsp (5 mL) lemon zest

2 Tbsp (30 mL) orange blossom honey

Salt and pepper to taste

1 head iceberg lettuce

1 large red onion, finely diced

2 cups (500 mL) frozen green peas, thawed

1 cucumber, thinly sliced

8 eggs, boiled and thinly sliced

1/2 cup (125 mL) Parmigiano-Reggiano shavings

1 Tbsp (15 mL) diced fresh Italian parsley

Tangy Macaroni Salad

Great for picnics and barbecues, this tangy salad is never-to-be-forgotten by your friends and family. On hot summer days, be mindful to keep this salad in the shade over ice.

Serves 6

1. In a medium skillet, cook pancetta over medium heat until crispy. Set aside.
2. In a 4-quart (4 L) pot halfway filled with water, combine salt, oil and pasta and stir. Bring to a boil and cook pasta until al dente, about 8–10 minutes.
3. Transfer pasta to a colander and drain, then transfer to a large bowl.
4. Add pancetta and all remaining ingredients and mix well. Cover with plastic wrap and refrigerate until ready to serve.

INGREDIENTS

1/2 cup (125 mL) diced pancetta or smoked ham
Salt to taste
3 Tbsp (45 mL) olive oil
3 cups (750 mL) elbow or rotini pasta (uncooked)
1/2 medium onion, diced
1/2 red bell pepper, diced
1/2 orange bell pepper, diced
2 Tbsp (30 mL) fresh lemon juice
1 cup (250 mL) mayonnaise
1/2 tsp (2 mL) Dijon mustard
1/2 cup (125 mL) sweet relish
1/2 Scotch bonnet pepper, finely diced
Salt and pepper to taste

Spinach, Hibiscus & Crabapple Salad with Creamy Soursop-Peppercorn Dressing

I grew up eating these fragrant apples straight off the tree. Crabapples are wild miniature apples with a sweet and sour flavor profile that pairs well with earthy green spinach, berry-rich hibiscus (same family as okra), and peppery arugula in this salutary salad.

Serves 4

1. In a small glass bowl, combine diced apples and lemon juice and toss.
2. In a large salad bowl, combine spinach, hibiscus and arugula and toss.
3. Add apples over salad with walnuts. Serve drizzled with dressing.

   TIP: For a special treat, add Herbed Johnny Cake Croutons (see recipe, page 13)

INGREDIENTS

2 crabapples or Gala apples, cored and diced
2 Tbsp (30 mL) lemon juice
4 cups (1 L) prewashed spinach leaves
4 colorful edible hibiscus leaves torn
1 cup (250 mL) rocket arugula
1/2 cup (125 mL) toasted chopped walnuts
1 cup (250 mL) Creamy Soursop-Peppercorn Dressing (see recipe, page 11)

Bahama Summer Rice Salad

Aromatic jasmine and earthy wild rice are combined in this fruity and vibrantly flavored salad, guaranteed to delight the palate.
Serves 6

1. In a large bowl, combine jasmine and wild rice and mix. Add remaining ingredients and mix well.

   TIP: Serve as an accompaniment to roast chicken, pork and seafood; this recipe is also great as a side dish at a barbecue.

INGREDIENTS

4 cups (1 L) cooked jasmine rice
1 cup (250 mL) cooked wild rice
1/2 medium red onion, diced
2 stalks celery, diced
2 tsp (10 mL) lemon zest
1/2 yellow bell pepper, diced
1/2 cup (125 mL) diced apricots
1/2 cup (125 mL) dried cherries
1/2 cup (125 mL) pecan pieces, toasted
1/4 cup (60 mL) diced fresh
   Italian parsley
2 cups (500 mL) Mango Passion
   Vinaigrette (see recipe, page 10)

Drum "Beet" Salad

I love the earthy flavor of beets as much as I enjoy the rhythm of the goat skin drums at The Bahamas world renowned Junkanoo Festivals. In this recipe, I use a combination of fresh red and naturally sweet golden beets complemented with Mango Passion Vinaigrette.

Serves 10

1. Preheat the oven to 400°F (200°C).
2. Wash and keep golden and red beets separate; place onto two 8-inch (20 cm) square baking sheets.
3. Add 1/2 cup (125 mL) water, olive oil and thyme sprigs to each pan and season with salt and pepper. Cover with foil and bake in the oven until beets are tender when pierced with a knife, about 45 minutes.
4. Line a baking sheet with parchment paper. Remove beets and set aside on the baking sheets. Let cool enough to handle. Peel and discard the outer layers (keep beets separated as the red beets will stain the golden beets). Cut, the beets into desired shapes (wedges, diced or julienned) and set aside in a bowl.
5. In a small glass bowl, toss coconut with sugar and canola oil to caramelize for a hint of sweetness. Heat a skillet over medium heat and add the coconut rings. Cook on both sides until caramelized, about 1–2 minutes per side. Set aside.
6. To plate, cut out a piece of balsamic sheet with a cookie cutter or paring knife to fit a sheets or platter. Wash and dry frisée and position over the balsamic sheets. Position beets, mandarin, pomegranate and coconut over the sheets. Garnish with pieces of chèvre and parsley then drizzle with Mango Passion Vinaigrette. Serve at once.

INGREDIENTS

8 medium golden beets, stems removed

4 medium red beets, stems removed

3 Tbsp olive oil

3 sprigs fresh thyme

Salt and pepper to taste

1 cup (250 mL) coconut shavings or rings

1/4 cup (60 mL) confectioner's (icing) sugar

2 Tbsp (30 mL) canola oil

10 Balsamic sheets (see recipe, page 11)

3 heads frisée torn, tough outer stems removed

3 cups (750 mL) mandarin orange slices

1 cup (250 mL) fresh pomegranate seeds

1 cup (250 mL) chèvre (goat's milk cheese)

1/4 cup (60 mL) diced fresh Italian parsley

1 cup (250 mL) Mango Passion Vinaigrette (see recipe, page 10)

TIP: Fresh pomegranate seeds are sold already extracted from the pulp in supermarkets for your convenience. For guaranteed freshness, it is fairly easy to remove the seeds from the fruit by cutting it in half with a sharp knife, then placing it flesh side down in the palm of your hand over a small bowl (to catch the seeds); spread fingers apart while holding the pomegranate, hit the fruit with a wooden spoon to release the seeds.

CHAPTER 5

CASUAL DINING
Under The Sun,
Stars & By The Sea

- CHICKEN IN-DA-BAG
- STUFFED CHICKEN BAKED IN TAMARIND SAUCE
- JOHNNY CAKE CHICKEN POT PIE
- ISLAND CURRY CHICKEN WITH SWEET POTATOES
- GOOMBAY CHICKEN
- BROWN STEW CHICKEN
- SUNDAY ROAST CHICKEN & GRAVY
- FESTIVE JERK CHICKEN DRUMSTICKS
- CARIBBEAN CREAM OF MUSHROOM CHICKEN
- FENNEL SPICED OVEN-FRIED TURKEY
- STOVETOP TURKEY MEATLOAF
- CITRUS-GLAZED STUFFED CORNISH HENS
- LONG ISLAND BRAISED DUCK IN GUAVA RUM SAUCE
- CARIBBEAN ROAST PORK WITH PIKLIZ & CRACKLING
- GUAVA-BARBECUE BEEF RIBS
- TENDER STEAMED PORK CHOPS
- PORK CHOP SANDWICH WITH MUSTARD & CHILI-LIME MAYONNAISE
- AUNT TIA'S FESTIVE HOLIDAY HAM
- BRAISED OXTAILS WITH LIMA BEANS
- CURRY MUTTON WITH COCONUT MILK
- GRANDMA'S SENSATIONAL MEATLOAF

- LAMB CHOPS BAKED IN TOMATO SAUCE
- AROMATIC BRAISED LAMB SHANKS
- BAHAMA ROCK MINCED LOBSTER
- EXUMA CRACKED CONCH
- ABACO STEAMED CONCH
- NASSAU GROUPER FINGERS
- BAHAMA GRILLED GROUPER IN PARCHMENT
- EARTHY MOROS (CUBAN RICE & BEANS)
- RICE & PEAS
- DIRI AK DJON DJON (RICE WITH MUSHROOMS)
- PEAS & RICE WITH COCONUT OIL
- RUM CAY PEAS & GRITS WITH CONCH
- CURRIED RICE
- STEAMED COCONUT JASMINE RICE
- MAD MAC & CHEESE
- SWEET POTATO MASH
- ROASTED SAGE & GARLIC MASHED CASSAVAS
- FENNEL SPICED CABBAGE
- SWITCHA ROOT VEGETABLES
- ROASTED CORN WITH MAPLE-CHILE DRESSING
- SAUTÉED CALLALOO
- BAKED BLACK-EYED PEAS
- SPICED POPCORN CAULIFLOWER

CHICKEN-IN-DA-BAG

Chicken-in-the-bag is as native to The Bahamas as Jerk is to Jamaica. There are many take-away "chicken shacks" located throughout The Bahamas, and this crispy golden fried chicken is best when seasoned with a proprietor's special family-blend of spices and served with hand cut fries (and ketchup and hot sauce) and a homemade dinner roll. And yes, it's served in a paper bag. So plan to experience the tastiest island fried chicken the next time you visit.

Serves 4

1. Preheat a deep fryer with oil to 350°F (180°C).
2. In a medium bowl, combine cut potatoes with cold water for crispier fries. Set aside.
3. Trim any excess fat from chicken and rinse in a large bowl of cold water and 1 Tbsp (15 mL) white vinegar; pat dry with paper towels. Return chicken parts to the bowl. Add lime juice, orange juice and season with 1/4 cup (60 mL) seasoned salt. Set aside.
4. In another large bowl, add buttermilk. Whisk in eggs, then 1 1/2 cups (375 mL) flour to form a smooth batter. Add pepper sauce and salt and stir.
5. Transfer seasoned chicken parts to the buttermilk mixture. In a large plastic food bag, combine 4 cups (1 L) remaining flour and black pepper and set aside.
6. Meanwhile, line a baking sheet with paper towels and set aside. Dry fries in a towel and transfer to the basket of the deep fryer and fry until golden, about 5–6 minutes. Transfer fries to the baking sheet and immediately season fries with remaining 1/4 cup (60 mL) of seasoning salt and keep warm.

continued on page 138

INGREDIENTS

Canola or vegetable oil

4 Idaho potatoes, cut into fries

3–4 lb (1.4–1.8 kg) whole chicken, quartered

1 Tbsp (15 mL) white vinegar

1/4 cup (60 mL) fresh lime juice

1/4 cup (60 mL) fresh orange juice

1/2 cup (125 mL) Raquel's Seasoned Salt (see recipe, page 2), divided

2 cups (500 mL) buttermilk

2 eggs, lightly beaten

1 1/2 cups (375 mL) + 4 cups (1 L) all-purpose flour, divided

2 Tbsp (30 mL) Caribbean pepper sauce

1/2 tsp (2 mL) salt

1 tsp (5 mL) freshly ground black pepper

4 sweet rolls

2 cups (500 mL) Island Currant Ketchup (see recipe, page 8)

Hot sauce to taste

4 sprigs fresh thyme leaves

7. Remove chicken from the buttermilk mixture and add to the plastic food bag with flour; shake to coat.
8. Place chicken in the basket of the deep fryer and fry until golden and an instant-read thermometer inserted into the thickest part of the meat registers 165°F (74°C).
9. To assemble, place a paper plate that fits in the bottom of a lunch paper bag, then place a piece of wax paper over the plate. Fold the bag down toward the plate, leaving the top open and exposing the plate. Place some of the fries on the plate and then a piece of golden fried chicken with the dinner roll. Garnish with ketchup, hot sauce and fragrant thyme sprig for presentation and serve at once.

Stuffed Chicken Baked in Tamarind Sauce

Impress your guests with this elegantly stuffed roasted chicken in a sweet-piquant tamarind sauce. Serve with Sweet Potato Mash and Switcha Root Vegetables (see recipes, pages 183 and 186).
Serves 4

1. Preheat oven to 400°F (200°C). Line a 13- x 9-inch (33 x 23 cm) roasting pan with parchment paper and set aside.
2. Rinse chicken in a large bowl with cold water and 1 Tbsp (15 mL) white vinegar. Pat dry with paper towels. Transfer to the roasting pan, skin side up, and pour dressing over top. Season with seasoned salt. Set aside.
3. In a large skillet, cook bacon over medium heat. Roughly chop and set aside on a plate lined with paper towels. Reserve fat in the skillet to cook vegetables.
4. Add onion, garlic and bell peppers to the skillet with bacon fat over medium heat and cook for 3 minutes. Transfer to a large bowl and add bacon and remaining ingredients for stuffing, adjust seasoning and mix well.
5. Place stuffing in the cavity of the chicken and dot with butter. Cover the cavity with foil.
6. Pour half of the Tamarind Glaze & Grill Sauce over stuffed chicken and transfer to the center rack of the oven. Bake, uncovered, basting halfway with the additional sauce, for 45 minutes or until an instant-read thermometer inserted into the thickest part of the meat registers 165°F (74°C).

INGREDIENTS

4–5 lb (1.8–2.2 kg) whole chicken
1 Tbsp (15 mL) white vinegar
1 cup (250 mL) Italian salad dressing
1/4 cup (60 mL) Raquel's Seasoned Salt (see recipe, page 2)

Stuffing
1/2 lb (225 g) hickory smoked bacon slices
1/2 medium onion, finely diced
4 cloves garlic, diced
1/4 cup (60 mL) diced green bell pepper
1/4 cup (60 mL) diced red bell pepper
1 cup (250 mL) diced prunes
1/4 cup (60 mL) diced fresh Italian parsley
1 Tbsp (15 mL) fresh thyme leaves
1/2 tsp (2 mL) ground sage
2 cups (500 mL) plain bread crumbs
1 cup (250 mL) panko bread crumbs
1 cup (250 mL) chicken stock
Salt and pepper to taste

1 Tbsp (15 mL) butter
2 cups (500 mL) Tamarind Glaze & Grilling Sauce, (see recipe, page 12), divided

Johnny Cake Chicken Pot Pie

I enjoy comfort foods immensely, and the classic chicken pot pie is chicken soup baked in a pastry crust. I've decided to put a Bahamian spin on it here with a divine Herbed Johnny Cake Crust—it's a gastronomical delight!

Serves 8

1. Preheat oven to 350˚F (180˚C). Set aside a 13- x 9-inch (33 x 23 cm) baking dish.
2. Make the crust for Aunt Tia's Johnny Cake. Roll dough 1/2 inch (1 cm) thick to fit inside the baking dish, leaving a 1/2-inch (1 cm) space at the edge of the pan (dough will spread while baking).
3. Mix herb toppings with cornstarch and set aside.
4. Rinse chicken in a large bowl with cold water and 1 Tbsp (15 mL) white vinegar. Pat dry with paper towels. Cut thighs into 1-inch (2.5 cm) pieces, then return to the bowl.
5. Pour lemon juice over chicken and season with seasoned salt. Set aside.
6. In an 8-quart (8 L) pot, heat oil and butter over medium heat. Add flour and stir for 1 minute. Add onion, garlic and celery and cook for 1 minute more until flour is bubbly.
7. Add milk while continuing to stir. Add wine and stock and bring to a boil. Add chicken with juices from bowl, potato, carrots and corn. Reduce heat and simmer; cover pot with a lid slightly ajar and cook, stirring occasionally, for 15 minutes.
8. Add peas, thyme, oregano, nutmeg and salt and pepper and cook, stirring, for 10 minutes more. Skim off any fat on the surface, adjust seasoning and remove from heat.

continued on page142

INGREDIENTS

Herbed Johnny Cake Crust
Aunt Tia's Johnny Cake (see Variation, page 34)

Herb Mix
1 Tbsp (15 mL) diced fresh
   Italian parsley
1 Tbsp (15 mL) diced fresh basil
2 tsp (10 mL) diced fresh chives
1 Tbsp (15 mL) cornstarch

Pot Pie Filling
3 1/2 lbs (1.6 kg) boneless skinless
   chicken thighs
1 Tbsp (15 mL) white vinegar
1/2 cup (125 mL) lemon juice
1/4 cup (60 mL) Raquel's Seasoned Salt
   (see recipe, page 2)
3 Tbsp (45 mL) olive oil
1/2 cup (125 mL) butter
2/3 cup (160 mL) all-purpose flour
1 large sweet onion, cut into 1-inch
   (2.5 cm) pieces
2 cloves garlic, diced
2 celery stalks, cut into
   1/2-inch (1 cm) pieces
4 cups (1 L) whole milk
1/2 cup (125 mL) white wine
2 1/2 cups (625 mL) chicken stock
1 large Caribbean sweet potato, diced

continued on page142

9. Ladle soup into the baking dish (reserve the leftover soup for plating), leaving 1/2-inch (1 cm) space at top for dough.

10. In a microwave-safe bowl, warm the cream in the microwave for 35 seconds.

11. Place dough over soup (if dough splits, it will come together while baking). Sprinkle herb mixture over top, then pour warm cream over the dough.

12. Set baking dish on a baking sheet and bake in oven, about 25 minutes. Serve at once in individual bowls, making sure to spoon the additional soup around the golden johnny cake crust.

2 large carrots, sliced 1/2-inch (1 cm) thick on the diagonal
2 ears corn, kernels removed
2 cups (500 mL) frozen peas, thawed
2 tsp (10 mL) fresh thyme leaves
2 tsp (10 mL) dried oregano
Pinch of nutmeg
Salt and pepper to taste

1/2 cup (125 mL) whipping (or heavy) cream (35%)

ISLAND CURRY CHICKEN WITH SWEET POTATOES

Sweet potatoes are usually labeled as yams. This couldn't be further from the truth though, as yams are related to palms and grasses while sweet potatoes belong to the morning glory family. Yams are cylindrical, dry, starchy and resemble the rough bark of a tree trunk, while sweet potatoes are sweet, moist and elongated in shape with tapered ends. I enjoy this superfood immensely and I usually combine more than one type of sweet potatoes in my recipes, as in this curry chicken dish.

Serves 6

1. Rinse chicken in a large bowl with cold water and 1 Tbsp (15 mL) white vinegar. Drain. Add 1/2 cup (125 mL) red vinegar and season parts with seasoned salt and 1/2 cup (125 mL) of the curry powder.
2. In a large skillet, heat 1/2 cup (125 mL) oil over medium heat. Add chicken parts and brown on both sides, about 3 minutes per side. Set aside on a large plate.
3. In an 8-quart (8 L) pot, heat remaining 3 Tbsp (45 mL) oil over medium heat. Add remaining curry powder and cook until fragrant for 3 minutes.
4. Add onion, garlic and ginger and cook for 2 minutes. Add potatoes and cook, stirring occasionally, for 2 minutes more.
5. Add tomatoes and cook for 2 minutes. Add bay leaf, thyme and hot stock and bring to a boil.
6. Add chicken along with remaining liquid in the bowl; add Scotch bonnet pepper and 1 Tbsp (15 mL) red wine vinegar and stir. Reduce heat to medium and cook for 30 minutes or until juices run clear when thighs are pierced. Skim oil from the top and adjust seasoning.

TIP: Serve with Steamed Coconut Jasmine Rice (see recipe, page 181), Exotic Coleslaw (see recipe, page 120) and plantain chips.

INGREDIENTS

3 lbs (1.4 kg) chicken parts (legs, thighs and wings)

1 Tbsp (15 mL) white vinegar

1/2 cup (125 mL) + 1 Tbsp (15 mL) red wine vinegar

1/4 cup (60 mL) Raquel's Seasoned Salt (see recipe, page 2)

1 cup (250 mL) Caribbean curry powder, divided

1/2 cup (125 mL) + 3 Tbsp (45 mL) canola oil, divided

1 medium onion, sliced

4 cloves garlic, diced

1 tsp (5 mL) minced ginger

1 large Caribbean sweet potato, diced (see page 223)

1 large orange-fleshed sweet potato, diced

1 cup (250 mL) diced tomatoes

1 bay leaf

1 Tbsp (15 mL) fresh thyme leaves

8 cups (2 L) chicken stock, heated

1 Scotch bonnet pepper, diced

Salt and pepper to taste

GoomBay Chicken

My inspiration for creating this vibrantly flavored recipe derives from a historic festival in The Bahamas called Goombay. It is a celebration of Bahamian music, dance, food, art and culture that was launched in 1974. Just as an artist is drawn to paint portraits from life's experiences, a chef's canvas is the kitchen, where masterful recipes are created. I pay homage to my childhood memories of Goombay summers with this zesty and luscious dish.

Serves 4

1. Rinse chicken in a large bowl with cold water and 1 Tbsp (15 mL) white vinegar. Pat dry with paper towels.
2. In a large bowl, add chicken, pour salad dressing over and season with seasoned salt.
3. In a large skillet, heat 1/2 cup (125 mL) of the garlic oil over medium-high heat. Add chicken parts and brown on both sides, about 3 minutes per side. Set aside on a plate.
4. In a wide-bottom 6-quart (6 L) pot, heat 3 Tbsp (45 mL) of the reserved garlic oil over medium heat.
5. Remove tough outer layers from lemongrass stalk and discard. Dice lemongrass and add to oil with onion and cook, stirring occasionally, for 3 minutes.
6. Add tomatoes and cook for 3 minutes more. Add ketchup and pineapple soda and stir. Add hot stock and bring to a boil.
7. Stir in bay leaf, Worcestershire sauce, browning, Scotch bonnet pepper and bring to a boil. Add chicken. Reduce heat to medium, cover with a lid that is slightly ajar, and cook for 25 minutes.
8. Add bell peppers and coconut cream. Adjust seasoning and cook for 15 minutes more, or until an instant-read thermometer inserted into the thickest part of the meat registers 165°F (74°C). Serve over rice. Drizzle Green Vinaigrette over GoomBay Chicken.

INGREDIENTS

1/2 cup (125 mL) Prepared Garlic Oil, see recipe on page 3

3–4 lb (1.4–1.8 kg) whole chicken, cut into quarters
1 Tbsp (15 mL) white vinegar
1 cup (250 mL) Italian salad dressing
1/4 cup (60 mL) Raquel's Seasoned Salt (see recipe, page 2)
1 lemongrass stalk
1 medium sweet onion, sliced
2 cups (500 mL) diced tomatoes
1/2 cup (125 mL) ketchup
1 cup (250 mL) pineapple soda
2 cups (500 mL) chicken stock, heated
1 bay leaf
1 Tbsp (15 mL) Worcestershire sauce
1 tsp (5 mL) browning (see page 219)
1 Scotch bonnet pepper, finely diced
1 carrot, cut into 1/4-inch (6 mm) pieces on the diagonal
1 red bell pepper, julienned
1/2 each yellow and orange bell pepper, julienned
1 cup (250 mL) coconut cream
Salt and pepper to taste
Cooked jasmine rice
1 cup (250 mL) Green Vinaigrette (see recipe, page 4)

Brown Stew Chicken

There can never be too many exceptional chicken recipes, and this savory, piquant dish is no exception. It's not your regular roux-based stew but a scrumptious tangy gravy with flavorful and tender spiced chicken that screams "eat me!" Serve with Rice & Peas (see recipe, page 175) and Sautéed Callaloo (see recipe, page 188).

Serves 6

1. Rinse chicken in a large bowl with cold water and 1 Tbsp (15 mL) white vinegar. Pat dry with paper towels.
2. In a large bowl, add chicken and pour red wine vinegar over; season with seasoned salt and black pepper. Add remaining marinade ingredients and rub all over the chicken. Refrigerate for 1 hour.
3. To prepare the brown gravy, in a skillet, heat 1/2 cup (125 mL) oil over medium heat. Remove any green onions or garlic from the chicken parts and brown chicken on both sides, about 3 minutes per side. Set aside on a plate, reserving the juices in the bowl.
4. In a 4-quart (4 L) wide-bottomed pot, heat 3 Tbsp (45 mL) oil over medium heat. Add onion and green and red bell peppers and cook for 3 minutes. Stir in reserved juices and ketchup.
5. Add stock and bring to a boil. Stir in browning, brown sugar and thyme. Add chicken and cover with a lid that is slightly ajar. Reduce heat and simmer for 30 minutes or until an instant-read thermometer inserted into the thickest part of the meat registers 165°F (74°C).
6. Add paprika, green onions and Scotch bonnet pepper and cook for 5 minutes more. Adjust seasoning and serve at once with Rice & Peas and Sautéed Callaloo.

INGREDIENTS

3 lbs (1.4 kg) chicken thighs
1 Tbsp (15 mL) white vinegar

Marinade
1/4 cup (60 mL) red wine vinegar
1/3 cup (80 mL) Raquel's Seasoned Salt (see recipe, page 2)
1 tsp (5 mL) freshly ground black pepper
1 Tbsp (15 mL) brown sugar
2 tsp (10 mL) diced fresh ginger
6 cloves garlic, diced
2 tsp (10 mL) fresh thyme leaves
1 chicken bouillon cube, crushed into powder
3 green onions, mashed and thinly sliced on the diagonal
1 Tbsp (15 mL) Maggi seasoning sauce
2 Tbsp (30 mL) browning (see page 219)

Brown Gravy
1/2 cup (125 mL) + 3 Tbsp (45 mL) canola oil
1 medium onion, sliced
1/2 green bell pepper, diced
1/2 red bell pepper, diced
1/4 cup (60 mL) ketchup
4 cups (1 L) chicken stock, heated
2 tsp (10 mL) browning
1 Tbsp (15 mL) brown sugar
2 tsp (10 mL) fresh thyme leaves
1 tsp (5 mL) paprika
3 green onions, thinly sliced diagonal
1 Scotch bonnet pepper, diced
Salt and pepper to taste

Sunday Roast Chicken & Gravy

Sunday dinners are a Bahamian tradition where we look forward to enjoying celebratory meals, while eating together and bonding with friends and family. These dinners usually start in the afternoon and continue until late evenings. A scrumptious and succulent chicken dish is always well received as one of the proteins on display at Sunday dinners.

Serves 4

1. Preheat the oven to 400°F (200°C).
2. Rinse chicken in a large bowl with cold water and 1 Tbsp (15 mL) white vinegar. Pat dry with paper towels.
3. Line a 13- x 9-inch (33 x 23 cm) roasting pan with parchment paper and place chicken on top, skin side up, in pan. Pour salad dressing over chicken. Add coriander and seasoned salt and mix. Season chicken with seasoned salt mixture.
4. Place 4 of the garlic cloves inside the cavity of the chicken. Combine remaining 4 garlic cloves, onion, carrots and potatoes and position around chicken. Place 1 rosemary sprig inside the cavity of chicken and remaining sprigs on top of the vegetables.
5. In a small bowl, combine sauce ingredients. Pour half of the sauce over the chicken. Cover loosely with foil and cook for 30 minutes.
6. Remove pan from oven and discard foil. Remove the cooked vegetables and set aside on a plate and keep warm. Carefully drain and discard the pan's juices and return, uncovered, to the oven. Spoon remaining sauce over chicken and continue to roast, basting occasionally, about 15–20 minutes more or until an instant-read thermometer inserted into the thickest part of the meat registers 165°F (75°C).
7. Transfer chicken to a platter with the roasted vegetables. Cut and discard the butcher's twine and serve with gravy on the side.

INGREDIENTS

4–5 1b (1.8–2.2 kg) whole chicken, trussed
1 Tbsp (15 mL) white vinegar
1/4 cup (60 mL) Italian salad dressing
1 tsp (5 mL) ground coriander
1/4 cup (60 mL) Raquel's Seasoned Salt (see recipe, page 2)
8 garlic cloves, divided
1 large onion, quartered
1 1b (450 g) baby carrots
2 lbs (1 kg) fingerling potatoes, cut in half lengthwise
3 sprigs rosemary leaves

Sauce

1/4 cup (60 mL) Worcestershire sauce
1/2 cup (125 mL) balsamic vinegar
2 Tbsp (30 mL) Maggi liquid seasoning
2 Tbsp (30 mL) browning (see page 219)
1/4 tsp (1 mL) freshly ground black pepper

TIP: Cover the chicken by making a dome shape with foil over the pan before placing it in the oven. This will prevent the foil from any contact with the chicken while roasting.

Festive Jerk Chicken Drumsticks

Although this dish originates from Jamaica, Bahamians have adopted it into their culture. On any given day, you could see and smell the smoke emanating from a jerk hut throughout the Bahamas.

Serves 6

1. Fire up the grill to medium heat. Rinse chicken in a large bowl with cold water and 1 Tbsp (15 mL) white vinegar. Pat dry with paper towels.
2. Pour red wine vinegar over chicken and season with salt. Add oil and rub over chicken. Set aside.
3. In the bowl of a food processor, add remaining ingredients for the rub and purée. Using food safety gloves, rub half of the mixture all over the legs. Reserve remaining rub for the sauce.
4. To prepare the jerk sauce, in a 1-quart (1 L) saucepan, add remaining jerk rub and water and stir over medium heat. Bring to a boil. Add ketchup and Scotch bonnet pepper. Reduce heat and simmer, about 10-15 minutes or until sauce is slightly thickened to coat the back of a spoon. Taste and adjust with sugar if the sauce is too spicy. Remove from heat and transfer to a small bowl.
5. Place chicken on grill and cook on both sides until an instant-read thermometer inserted into the thicket part of the meat registers 165˚F (74˚C).
6. Transfer chicken to a platter and spoon sauce over top. Serve with Rice & Peas (see recipe, page 175) and Caribbean Mango Salsa.

TIP: For maximum flavor, prepare the jerk rub and marinate the chicken in the refrigerator overnight.

INGREDIENTS

Jerk Rub
3 lbs (1.4 kg) chicken legs (drumsticks)
1 Tbsp (15 mL) white vinegar
1/2 cup (125 mL) red wine vinegar
1/4 cup (60 mL) Raquel's Seasoned Salt
   (see recipe, page 2)
1/4 cup (60 mL) olive oil
1/2 large onion, cut in half
2 Tbsp (30 mL) whole allspice, crushed
1-inch (2.5 cm) piece ginger,
   with skin on
1 bay leaf
6 cloves garlic
1/4 cup (60 mL) green onions, sliced
2 Scotch bonnet peppers, cut in half
1 tsp (5 mL) brown sugar
1 Tbsp (15 mL) fresh thyme leaves
2 tsp (10 mL) smoked paprika
2 Tbsp (30 mL) browning (see page 219)

Jerk Sauce
1/2 of the Jerk Rub
2 cups (500 mL) water
1/4 cup (60 mL) ketchup
1 Scotch bonnet pepper, finely diced
1 tsp (5 mL) brown sugar (optional)
Rice & Peas (see recipe, page 178)
Caribbean Mango Salsa (see recipe,
   page 9)

CARIBBEAN CREAM OF MUSHROOM CHICKEN

I have fond memories of this cream of mushroom chicken recipe, as this was the meal that my hubby prepared for me on our first date. I was impressed by his efforts and over the years we have perfected this modest and tasty dish to an enticing meal with an island flare by adding coconut cream.

Serves 6

1. Preheat oven to 375°F (190°C). Line a 13- x 9-inch (33 x 23 cm) baking dish with parchment paper and set aside.
2. Rinse chicken in a large bowl with cold water and 1 Tbsp (15 mL) white vinegar. Pat dry with paper towels.
3. Pour salad dressing over chicken and season with seasoned salt. Transfer chicken to the baking dish and cover with foil. Bake in the oven for 30 minutes.
4. Meanwhile, in the bowl of a food processor, purée coconut cream, soup, half of the mushrooms, garlic, ginger and cayenne pepper. With the motor running, gradually pour in stock.
5. Remove baking dish from the oven and pour off any excess liquid.
6. Pour soup mixture over the chicken. Cover the chicken with remaining mushrooms, bell pepper and parsley. Cover chicken loosely with foil and bake for 15 minutes more. Uncover and bake for 5 minutes more.

TIPS: Serve over jasmine rice with a side of Spinach, Hibiscus & Crabapple Salad (see recipe, page 128).

This recipe could also be prepared on the stovetop by browning the chicken in a large skillet after seasoning. Cook in a 6-quart (6 L) pot over medium heat by following steps 4 and 6, covering the pot with a lid slightly ajar and cooking for about 30 minutes until done.

INGREDIENTS

6 chicken legs with thighs attached
1 Tbsp (15 mL) white vinegar
1 cup (250 mL) Italian salad dressing
1/2 cup (125 mL) Raquel's Seasoned Salt (see recipe, page 2)
2 cups (500 mL) coconut cream
4 cups (1 L) cream of chicken soup
3 cups (750 mL) sliced cremini or shiitake mushrooms, divided
4 cloves garlic, peeled and smashed
1 tsp (5 mL) minced ginger
1/4 tsp (1 mL) cayenne pepper
1/2 cup (125 mL) chicken stock
1/4 cup (60 mL) diced red bell pepper
1 Tbsp (15 mL) diced fresh Italian parsley

Fennel Spiced Oven-Fried Turkey

This is an essential dish for the holiday. Some people dislike turkey because it's lean and sometimes dry due to overcooking. You'll fall in love with turkey after sampling this aromatic, crispy-skinned and succulent poultry. No oil necessary, and it's guaranteed to be "the pièce de résistance" of the buffet.

Serves 15

1. If turkey is frozen, thaw overnight in the refrigerator.
2. Rinse turkey in a bowl of cold water and 1 Tbsp (15 mL) white vinegar. Pat dry with paper towels.
3. In a small bowl, combine fine sea salt and baking soda and pat generously over the top and side skin of the turkey. Season inside the cavity only with seasoned salt. Refrigerate for 2 hours.
4. Meanwhile, in a medium skillet, add fennel seeds and cardamom pods and toast over medium heat until light brown and fragrant, about 2 minutes. Remove from heat. Let cool and break cardamom pods with a pestle or mallet and remove seeds, discarding pods. Transfer fennel and cardamom seeds to a spice grinder and grind together.
5. In a small dish, combine ground spice seeds, ground coriander and pepper and mix. Set aside.
6. Preheat oven to 375°F (190°C). Remove turkey from the refrigerator. Carefully dust off skin with paper towels to remove most of the salt mixture. Lightly rub spice mixture all over the skin of the turkey.
7. Line a roasting pan with parchment paper and place turkey inside. Transfer to the center rack of the oven and bake for 2 hours or until an instant-read thermometer inserted into the thickest part of the thigh registers 165°F (74°C) and skin is golden and crispy. Place on a platter accompanied with gravy and cranberry sauce.

INGREDIENTS

15 lb (6.8 kg) whole young turkey
1 Tbsp (15 mL) white vinegar
1 cup (250 mL) fine sea salt
1 Tbsp (15 mL) baking soda
1/4 cup (60 mL) Raquel's Seasoned Salt (see recipe, page 2)
1/4 cup (60 mL) fennel seeds
1 Tbsp (15 mL) green cardamom pods
1 tsp (5 mL) ground coriander
1/4 tsp (1 mL) freshly ground black pepper
Home-style Peppercorn Gravy (see recipe, page 16)
Citrus Cranberry Sauce (see recipe, page 17)

TIP: For a celebratory meal serve with Sweet Potato Mash (see recipe, page 183) and Switcha Root Vegetables (see recipe, page 186).

STOVETOP TURKEY MEATLOAF

This rustic and zesty meatloaf features coarsely cut vegetables as "the star of the show." It's a mama's meatloaf that I inherited from my mother-in-law, a family treasure.
Serves 6

1. In a large bowl, combine turkey, seasonings, thyme, seasoned salt, eggs and 1/2 cup (125 mL) ketchup and mix thoroughly with hands.
2. Add all vegetables and plain and panko bread crumbs and mix. Form meatloaf into a round bun-like shape to fit inside a 4-quart (4 L) pot. Dust with flour on both sides.
3. In pot, heat oil over medium heat. Carefully add meatloaf and brown on each side for 3 minutes per side, flipping over with a large spatula (if it breaks apart, just push it back together with the spatula).
4. Pour tomatoes over and around the meatloaf. Cover with a lid that is slightly ajar and let cook, about 20–30 minutes or until an instant-read thermometer inserted into the center of the meat registers 165°F (74°C).
5. Add remaining ketchup and spoon tomato sauce over the meatloaf. Add parsley. Reduce heat to simmer and cook for 5 minutes more.
6. Pour half of the sauce onto a round platter and, using a spatula, carefully remove the meatloaf from the pot. Place over the sauce on the platter and spoon the additional sauce on top. Cut into wedges and serve with Roasted Sage & Garlic Mashed Cassavas.

TIP: For a tastier version, replace the ketchup with Island Currant Ketchup (see recipe, page 8).

INGREDIENTS

2 lbs (1 kg) ground turkey
2 tsp (10 mL) lemon pepper seasoning
2 tsp (10 mL) dried Italian seasoning
1 tsp (5 mL) thyme leaves
1 Tbsp (15 mL) Raquel's Seasoned Salt
2 eggs, lightly beaten
3/4 cup (190 mL) ketchup, divided
4 cloves garlic, diced
1 onion, diced
1 stalk celery, diced
1/2 red bell pepper, diced
1 carrot, grated coarsely
1 cup (250 mL) coarsely shredded
   savoy cabbage
1/2 cup (125 mL) coarsely shredded
   red cabbage
1 zucchini, julienned
1 squash, julienned
1 cup (250 mL) plain bread crumbs
1/2 cup (125 mL) panko bread crumbs
1/2 cup (125 mL) all-purpose flour
3 Tbsp (45 mL) olive oil
2 cups (500 mL) diced tomatoes
1 Tbsp (15 mL) diced fresh
   Italian parsley
Roasted Sage & Garlic Mashed
   Cassavas (see recipe, page 184)

CITRUS-GLAZED STUFFED CORNISH HENS

Here's the perfect recipe to prepare for a potluck dinner. This mouth-watering dish is appropriate for entertaining any day of the year and pairs well with just about any sides.

Serves 8

1. Preheat oven to 375°F (190°C). Line a 13 x 9-inch (33 x 23 cm) roasting pan with parchment paper and set aside.
2. Rinse hens in a large bowl with cold water and 1 Tbsp (15 mL) white vinegar. Pat dry with paper towels. Transfer to the roasting pan.
3. In a small bowl, combine salt, garlic powder, lemon pepper and thyme and mix. Rub spices over the hens. Place stuffing inside the cavities of the hens.
4. In a 1-quart (1 L) saucepan, melt butter over medium heat. Add juices and spices and mix well. Cook for 10 minutes or until sauce thickens slightly to coat the back of a spoon. Remove sauce from heat.
5. Pour half the sauce over the hens. Cover roasting pan with foil and bake in the oven for 30 minutes. Uncover and baste with remaining sauce and continue cooking for 15 minutes more, or until juices run clear in the leg when pierced. Serve at once.

INGREDIENTS

4 Cornish hens
1 Tbsp (15 mL) white vinegar
2 Tbsp (30 mL) fine sea salt
1 Tbsp (15 mL) garlic powder
2 tsp (10 mL) lemon pepper seasoning
1/2 tsp (2 mL) ground thyme
4 cups (1 L) stuffing (see recipe for Guava Spiced Stuffed Wings, page 82)
1/2 cup (125 mL) softened butter
2 cups (500 mL) frozen orange juice concentrate
1/2 cup (125 mL) frozen limeade juice concentrate
1/2 cup (125 mL) frozen mango juice concentrate
1/2 tsp (2 mL) ground cinnamon
1/4 tsp (1 mL) nutmeg
1 tsp (5 mL) smoked paprika

LONG ISLAND BRAISED DUCK IN GUAVA RUM SAUCE

Long Island is known as the most scenic island in The Bahamas with a population of over 3,000 inhabitants, and I pay homage to this picturesque island with this succulent and impressive recipe. Serve duck over Andros Native Grits (see recipe, page 37) or Sweet Potato Mash (see recipe, page 183).

Serves 6

1. Preheat oven to 350°F (180°C). Line a baking sheet with parchment paper and set aside.
2. Rinse duck in a large bowl with cold water and 1 Tbsp (15 mL) white vinegar. Pat dry with paper towels. Season with seasoned salt and refrigerate for 1 hour.
3. In an 8-quart (8 L) Dutch oven over high heat, combine salad dressing, duck (skin side up) and remaining ingredients (except Guava Rum Sauce) and bring to a boil, then cover tightly with a lid.
4. Carefully transfer pot to the oven and braise duck for 1 hour or until tender when pierced with a knife.
5. Meanwhile, to prepare the guava rum sauce, in a 1-quart (1 L) saucepan over medium heat, combine jam, barbecue sauce, lemon zest and juice and pepper and bring to a boil for 5 minutes. Stir in rum and cook for 3 minutes more. Set aside.
6. Remove pot from the oven and, using tongs, place duck legs on the baking sheet.
7. Adjust oven temperature to broil on high. Transfer baking sheet to the center rack in the oven and broil, about 1–2 minutes for a golden crispy skin.
8. Remove pan and spoon sauce over duck legs. Garnish with tarragon leaves and serve.

INGREDIENTS

6 duck leg quarters (thighs and legs attached)
1 Tbsp (15 mL) white vinegar
Salt and pepper
1/2 cup (125 mL) Raquel's Seasoned Salt (see recipe, page 2)
2 cups (500 mL) Italian salad dressing
4 cloves garlic, sliced
1/2 cup (125 mL) lightly packed brown sugar
1 Tbsp (15 mL) dried tarragon leaves
1 tsp (5 mL) dried basil
1 tsp (5 mL) dry mustard
4 cups (1 L) chicken stock, heated

Guava Rum Sauce
2 cups (500 mL) Guava Bell Pepper Jam (see recipe, page 10)
2 Tbsp (30 mL) barbecue sauce
1/2 lemon juice
2 tsp (10 mL) lemon zest
1/4 tsp (1 mL) freshly ground black pepper
1/2 cup (125 mL) spiced or dark rum

1 Tbsp (15 mL) diced fresh tarragon leaves, for garnish

CARIBBEAN ROAST PORK WITH PIKLIZ & CRACKLING

I've combined my aunt Marilyn's delectable five-hour slowly roasted pork dish with a tasty fusion of Cuban and Haitian ingredients. It's authentically Ba-cuban-aitian! I usually marinate the pork overnight in the refrigerator, place it in the oven at 9:00 am the following morning, then around 2:00 pm it's succulent, moist and ready for Sunday dinner. I can assure you that it's worth the wait! Serve with Earthy Moros (Cuban Rice & Black Beans (see recipe, page 174).
Serves 10

1. Preheat oven to 250°F (130°C). Set aside a 13- x 9-inch (33 x 23 cm) deep roasting pan.
2. Rinse pork (leg or shoulder) in a large bowl with cold water and 1 Tbsp (15 mL) white vinegar. Pat dry with paper towels. Pour lime and orange juices over the pork. In a small bowl, combine sea salt, cumin, garlic powder, smoked paprika, turmeric, oregano and pepper and rub over the pork.
3. Transfer pork with juices and marinade to the pan. Place garlic around the pork. Cover with foil and roast in oven for 5 hours, basting with the pan juices halfway during cooking.
4. To prepare the crackling, in a small bowl, mix together sea salt and baking soda. Dry pork belly with paper towels and place on a plate lined with paper towels.
5. Rub pork belly skin generously with seasoned salt mixture. Transfer to the bottom shelf in the refrigerator for about 2 hours or overnight.
6. Remove belly from the refrigerator and dust off salt with paper towels. Cut pork into 1-inch (2.5 cm) segments.
7. In a wide-bottom 7-quart (7 L) pot over high heat, add pork belly with just enough water to cover and bring to a boil. Reduce heat to low and simmer, turning pork occasionally (not allowing skin to stick to the bottom of the pot), about 2 hours or until water evaporates and lard forms. Continue to fry the pork segments in this lard, about 3 minutes until

INGREDIENTS

5 lbs (2.2 kg) pork leg or shoulder
1 Tbsp (15 mL) white vinegar
Juice of 6 limes
Juice of 3 oranges
1/4 cup (60 mL) fine sea salt
1 tsp (5 mL) ground cumin
1 Tbsp (15 mL) garlic powder
1/2 tsp (2 mL) smoked paprika
1 tsp (5 mL) ground turmeric
2 tsp (10 mL) dried oregano
1 tsp (5 mL) freshly ground black pepper
8 cloves garlic, sliced

Crackling
1/2 cup (125 mL) sea salt
1 Tbsp (15 mL) baking soda
2 1/2 lbs (1.1 kg) pork belly
1 Tbsp (15 mL) Raquel's Seasoned Salt (see recipe, page 2)

3 limes, cut into wedges
Pikliz (see recipe, page 86)

golden and crispy. Transfer to a plate lined with paper towels and season with seasoned salt.

8. To serve, slice tender pork leg and transfer to a platter. Spoon pan juices over top and garnish with lime wedges. Place cracklings over the pork. Serve with a side of pikliz.

TIP: It's imperative that you place a frying screen over the pan as pork fat splatters and could cause a severe burn. You may also fry the pork belly segments in the basket of a deep fryer, about 3 minutes until crispy and golden.

GUAVA-BARBECUE BEEF RIBS

Here's an alternative recipe for barbecue lovers with a tropical twist of guava; it's falling off the bone good! Serve with Roasted Corn with Maple Chili Dressing (see recipe, page 187) and Exotic Coleslaw (see recipe page 120).

Serves 6

1. Fire up the grill to high.
2. Season ribs on both sides with seasoned salt and set aside.
3. In an 8-quart (8 L) pot halfway filled with water, add garlic, berries, salad dressing, sugar and bay leaf and bring to a boil over high heat. Add ribs. Reduce heat to medium and simmer, about 90 minutes or until tender.
4. In a 1-quart (1 L) saucepan, add guava paste and 1/2 cup (125 mL) water over medium heat and mix, breaking up the paste until it is smooth with no lumps. Add remaining ingredients to make the guava-barbecue sauce and cook for 5 minutes. Remove from heat.
5. Transfer ribs to the hot grill and turn over until grill marks appear. Brush barbecue sauce generously on both sides. Transfer meat to a platter and serve.

INGREDIENTS

6 lbs (2.7 kg) beef ribs
1/2 cup (125 mL) Raquel's Seasoned Salt (see recipe, page 2)
6 cloves garlic, peeled and smashed
1 Tbsp (15 mL) crushed allspice berries
2 cups (500 mL) Italian salad dressing
1 cup (250 mL) lightly packed brown sugar
1 bay leaf
2 cups (500 mL) guava paste
2 cups (500 mL) barbecue sauce
1 Tbsp (15 mL) bourbon
1 Tbsp (15 mL) sambal oelek
1 tsp (5 mL) ground cinnamon
1/2 tsp (2 mL) freshly ground black pepper

TENDER STEAMED PORK CHOPS

I prefer the cut of pork chop ends for this native Bahamian recipe, as the fat content contributes to the savory umami flavor in this zesty recipe. Serve over Curried Rice (see recipe, page 180) or Sweet Potato Mash (see recipe, page 183).

Serves 8

1. Rinse pork chops in a large bowl with cold water and 1 Tbsp (15 mL) white vinegar. Pat dry with paper towels.
2. Pour red wine vinegar over chops and season with seasoned salt.
3. In a large skillet, heat canola oil over medium-high heat. Add chops and brown on both sides for 3 minutes per side. Transfer to a plate.
4. Reduce heat to medium, add olive oil to the skillet and heat. Add onion, garlic and bell pepper and cook for 3 minutes.
5. Add tomatoes and cook, stirring occasionally, for 5 minutes more. Stir in ketchup and stock and stir to make a gravy that coats the back of a spoon. Bring to a boil. Add chops and cook on high for 3 minutes.
6. Add remaining ingredients (except for the parsley). Reduce heat to low, cover with a lid that is slightly ajar and simmer, about 30–45 minutes or until tender and done.

INGREDIENTS

8 pork chops, bone-in
1 Tbsp (15 mL) white vinegar
1/2 cup (125 mL) red wine vinegar
1/4 cup (60 mL) Raquel's Seasoned Salt
  (see recipe, page 2)
1/2 cup (125 mL) canola oil
3 Tbsp (45 mL) olive oil
1/2 large sweet onion, sliced
4 cloves garlic, diced
1/2 green bell pepper, diced
2 medium ripe tomatoes, diced
1/2 cup (125 mL) ketchup
2 cups (500 mL) chicken stock, heated
1 Tbsp (15 mL) fresh thyme leaves
1 bay leaf
3 Tbsp (45 mL) Worcestershire sauce
1 Tbsp (15 mL) molasses
1 1/2 Scotch bonnet pepper, diced
Salt and pepper to taste
1 Tbsp (15 mL) diced fresh Italian
  parsley, for garnish

PORK CHOP SANDWICH WITH MUSTARD & CHILI LIME MAYONNAISE

This extraordinary sandwich is for pork lovers.

Serves 4

1. Preheat oven to 350°F (180°C). Line a baking sheet with parchment paper and set aside.
2. To make the pickled-onion relish, in a large skillet over medium heat, add garlic oil, then combine all other relish ingredients and simmer for 5 minutes. Remove from heat and store in a sterilized jar or a small dish. Add oil and cover with a lid. Store in the refrigerator for up to 1 week.
3. Rinse pork in a large bowl with cold water and 1 Tbsp (15 mL) white vinegar. Pat dry with paper towels.
4. Pour red wine vinegar over the chops and season with seasoned salt. Transfer to the baking sheet and drizzle with garlic oil. Cover with foil and bake in the oven for about 30 minutes. Discard foil.
5. Meanwhile, in a small bowl, mix half of the mayonnaise with honey and spoon over the pork while in the oven. Bake for 5 minutes more.
6. To assemble the sandwiches, generously spread remaining mayonnaise equally over 4 slices of bread. Divide lettuce, pork chops, cheese, tomato and onion relish over slices. Add a few drops of hot sauce, if using, and top with the remaining slices of bread. Serve at once with Exotic Chips.

INGREDIENTS

Pickled-Onion Relish

1 large red onion, sliced into rings
2 Tbsp (30 mL) diced ginger
1 tsp (5 mL) ground cumin
2 chadon beni leaves, diced
1/4 tsp (1 mL) salt
1/4 tsp (1 mL) freshly ground black pepper
2 cups (500 mL) cider vinegar
2 Tbsp (30 mL) Garlic Oil (see recipe, page 3)

4 pork chops, center cut and boneless
1 Tbsp (15 mL) white vinegar
1/2 cup (125 mL) red wine vinegar
3 Tbsp (45 mL) Raquel's Seasoned Salt (see recipe, page 2)
3 Tbsp (45 mL) Garlic Oil (see recipe, page 3)
2 cups (500 mL) Mustard & Chili Lime Mayonnaise (see recipe, page 12), divided
2 Tbsp (30 mL) honey
1 loaf coconut or egg bread, thickly sliced into 8 slices and lightly toasted
6 slices butter lettuce or leaf lettuce
6 slices smoked cheddar cheese
4 slices beef steak tomatoes
Hot sauce (optional)
Exotic Chips (see recipe page 16)

AUNT TIA'S FESTIVE HOLIDAY HAM

The holidays wouldn't be the same without my aunt's enchanting and luscious ham. Her bourbon glaze is the perfect flavor to complement smoked ham.

Serves 15

1. Preheat oven to 325°F (165°C). Line a 15- x 12-inch (38 x 30 cm) deep roasting pan with parchment paper and set aside.
2. Rinse ham in cold water. Transfer to a cutting board and using a sharp paring knife, score the top into diamonds. Stud the center of each diamond with a clove, then transfer to the pan.
3. In a small bowl, combine remaining ingredients (except pineapple and cherries). Pour half over ham. Cover with foil and bake, basting occasionally, for 90 minutes.
4. Remove ham from the oven after 1 hour. Spread pineapple chunks, cherries and remaining whiskey mixture over the ham and bake, uncovered, basting occasionally, for remaining 30 minutes.
5. Transfer ham to a platter to serve.

INGREDIENTS

15 lb (6.8 kg) smoked ham
1 Tbsp (15 mL) whole cloves
2 tsp (10 mL) ground cloves
1 cup (250 mL) whiskey
4 cups (1 L) Coca Cola
1 tsp (5 mL) ground cinnamon
1 tsp (5 mL) allspice
2 cups (500 mL) lightly packed
   brown sugar
2 cups (500 mL) pineapple
   chunks, drained
1 cup (250 mL) maraschino cherries

Braised Oxtails with Lima Beans

Our traditional Sunday dinners would not be the same without a scrumptious, falling-off-the-bone oxtail dish. Serve over Steamed Coconut Jasmine Rice (see recipe, page 181) and accompany with Fennel-Spiced Cabbage (see recipe, page 185).

Serves 6

1. Preheat oven to 350°F (180°C).
2. Trim any excess fat from oxtails and rinse in a large bowl of cold water and 1 Tbsp (15 mL) white vinegar. Drain and season with seasoned salt.
3. In a 6-quart (6 L) Dutch oven over high heat, add oxtails and remaining oxtail ingredients. Add water to cover meat. Cover pot with a lid and bring to a boil. Transfer to the oven and braise for 1 hour. Drain oxtails.
4. In a wide-bottomed 6-quart (6 L) pan, heat 1/4 cup (60 mL) oil over medium-high heat. Add browning sauce and brown oxtails, in batches, about 5 minutes per batch.
5. Add 3 Tbsp (45 mL) oil to the pot and reduce heat to medium. Add onion, garlic and bell pepper and cook for 3 minutes.
6. Add tomatoes and cook for 2 minutes. Stir in ketchup and stock and bring to a boil. Add oxtails and remaining ingredients. Cover with a lid that is slightly ajar and cook, stirring occasionally, for 15 minutes more.

INGREDIENTS

Braised Oxtails

3 lbs (1.4 kg) oxtails
1 Tbsp (15 mL) white vinegar
1/4 cup (60 mL) Raquel's Seasoned Salt (see recipe, page 2)
4 cups (1 L) beef stock
1/2 cup (125 mL) red wine vinegar
8 cloves garlic, sliced
1 Tbsp (15 mL) crushed allspice berries
1 bay leaf
1 whole Scotch bonnet pepper

1/4 cup (60 mL) + 3 Tbsp (45 mL) canola oil, divided
2 Tbsp (30 mL) + 1 tsp (5 mL) browning (see page 219)
1 medium sweet onion, sliced
6 cloves garlic, sliced
1/2 green bell pepper, diced
1 cup (250 mL) diced tomatoes
1/2 cup (125 mL) ketchup
4 cups (1 L) beef stock
3 Tbsp (45 mL) Worcestershire sauce
3 sprigs fresh thyme leaves
1 Scotch bonnet pepper, diced
2 cups (500 mL) cooked large lima beans
1/4 cup (60 mL) parsley, diced
Salt and pepper to taste

Curry Mutton with Coconut Milk

Braising is the perfect cooking method for mutton (sheep's meat after one year of age), as it's quite tough with a wonderful gamy flavor. Curry flavors assist by toning the gaminess with fragrant and elusive spices for a mouthwatering dish.

Serves 6

1. Preheat oven to 350°F (180°C).
2. Rinse meat in a large bowl of cold water and 1 Tbsp (15 mL) white vinegar. Drain.
3. Add vinaigrette to the bowl and rub over the meat. Season with seasoned salt. Add tomatoes, ketchup, green onions, allspice and half of the curry powder; mix with a spoon to coat the meat.
4. In a 6-quart (6 L) Dutch oven, heat oil over medium heat. Add remaining curry powder and cumin and cook for 3 minutes to release the fragrant oils.
5. Add onion and garlic and cook for 2 minutes more. Add 1 cup (250 mL) water and continue to cook, stirring occasionally, for 5 minutes. As the water evaporates the oil from the curry will be visible; increase heat to high and add marinated meat, a few pieces at a time, while stirring each batch.
6. Stir in thyme, Scotch bonnet pepper, vinegar and potatoes. Cover tightly with a lid and transfer to the oven to braise for 1 hour.
7. Carefully remove pot from the oven and place over high heat on the stovetop to burn off the natural juices released from the meat.
8. After liquid evaporates, add stock and coconut milk and continue to cook, stirring occasionally, for 30 minutes. Season to taste with salt and pepper. Serve topped with Green Mango Chutney and a side of rice.

INGREDIENTS

3 lbs (1.4 kg) mutton meat

1 Tbsp (15 mL) white vinegar

1 cup (250 mL) Green Vinaigrette (see recipe, page 4)

1/2 cup (125 mL) Raquel's Seasoned Salt (see recipe, page 2)

2 cups (500 mL) diced tomatoes

1/4 cup (60 mL) ketchup

1/4 bunch green onions, sliced roughly on the diagonal

1 Tbsp (15 mL) cracked allspice berries

1/2 cup (125 mL) Caribbean curry powder, divided

1/4 cup (60 mL) vegetable oil

1 tsp (5 mL) ground cumin

1/2 large sweet onion, sliced

4 cloves garlic, sliced

6 sprigs dried thyme leaves

1 Scotch bonnet pepper, diced

2 Tbsp (30 mL) red wine vinegar

2 russet potatoes, diced

2 cups (500 mL) chicken stock, heated

2 cups (500 mL) coconut milk

Salt and pepper to taste

2 cups (500 mL) Green Mango Chutney (see recipe, page 6)

Steamed Coconut Jasmine Rice (see recipe, page 181)

Grandma's Sensational Meatloaf

Nobody does meatloaf better than grandma! The ratio of ground beef and pork gives this meatloaf a savory texture that, along with the sweet and tangy sauce, elevates this dish to another level of remarkable comfort food. Serve over mashed potatoes or Roasted Sage & Garlic Mashed Cassavas (see recipe, page 184).

Serves 8

1. Preheat oven to 350°F (180°C).
2. In a large skillet, heat oil over medium heat. Add garlic and half of the onion, celery, green and red peppers and carrots and cook for 3 minutes (reserve the remaining half of vegetables for the sauce).
3. In a large bowl, add beef and pork and season with seasoned salt. Add cooked vegetables and mix with your hands.
4. Add tomato purée, eggs, black pepper, thyme and parsley and mix well.
5. Transfer meat mixture to a 13- x 9-inch (33 x 23 cm) baking dish and spread out evenly. Bake in the oven for 45 minutes or until an instant-read thermometer inserted in the center of the meat registers an internal temperature of 160°F (71°C).
6. In a 1-quart (1 L) saucepan over medium heat, add ketchup, jam and remaining vegetables with 1 cup (250 mL) of water and cook, stirring, about 10 minutes or until the sauce is slightly thickened to coat the back of a spoon.
7. When meatloaf has been baking for 40 minutes, pour sauce over the meatloaf and bake for the last 5 minutes.

INGREDIENTS

3 Tbsp (45 mL) olive oil
4 garlic cloves, diced
1 medium onion, diced, divided
2 celery stalks, diced, divided
1/2 green bell pepper, diced, divided
1/2 red bell pepper, diced, divided
2 carrots, diced
1 lb (450 g) ground beef
1 lb (450 g) ground pork
1 Tbsp (15 mL) Raquel's Seasoned Salt (see recipe, page 2)
1 cup (250 mL) tomato purée
2 eggs, slightly beaten
1/4 tsp (1 mL) freshly ground black pepper
3 sprigs fresh thyme leaves
1 Tbsp (15 mL) diced fresh Italian parsley
1 cup (250 mL) ketchup
1/2 cup (125 mL) guava jam or paste

Lamb Chops Baked in Tomato Sauce

If you love lamb as much as I do, you're always searching for exceptional recipes. I inherited this recipe from my mother-in-law, who was an expert on using suitable ingredients to soften the gamy taste of lamb. Serve with Curried Rice and Vangie's Broccoflower Salad (see recipes, pages 180 and 124).

Serves 6

1. Preheat oven to 375°F (190°C). Line a 13- x 9-inch (33 x 23 cm) metal baking pan with parchment paper and set aside.
2. Rinse meat in a large bowl of cold water and 1 Tbsp (15 mL) white vinegar. Drain and pat dry with paper towels.
3. Pour balsamic vinegar over meat and put in the garlic. In a small bowl, combine salt, garlic powder, cumin, cinnamon, Italian seasoning and rosemary. Rub over both sides of meat. Add oil and rub again.
4. In a medium bowl, combine tomato sauce and honey. Transfer meat to the pan and pour sauce over the meat. Top with onion rings. Cover with foil and bake in the oven for 30 minutes. Uncover and bake for 5 minutes more.

INGREDIENTS

6 lamb chops
1 Tbsp (15 mL) white vinegar
1/2 cup (125 mL) balsamic vinegar
1 Tbsp (15 mL) minced garlic
2 Tbsp (30 mL) fine sea salt
1 Tbsp (15 mL) garlic powder
1 tsp (5 mL) ground cumin
1 tsp (5 mL) ground cinnamon
2 tsp (10 mL) Italian seasoning
2 sprigs fresh rosemary leaves
3 Tbsp (45 mL) olive oil
2 cups (500 mL) Homemade Tomato
  Sauce (see recipe, page 8)
2 Tbsp (30 mL) honey
1 large red onion, sliced into rings
1 Tbsp (15 mL) diced fresh
  Italian parsley

Aromatic Braised Lamb Shanks

Over the years, lamb and mint jelly (or sauce) have been routinely paired together by cooks. It's really not the only condiment for lamb. In this recipe, sweet and tangy tamarind is the primary flavor that complements this luscious lamb. Serve with Switcha Root Vegetables (see recipe, page 186).

Serves 4

1. Preheat oven to 350°F (180°C). Line a 13- x 9-inch (33 x 23 cm) metal baking pan with parchment paper and set aside.
2. Rinse meat in a large bowl of cold water and 1 Tbsp (15 mL) white vinegar. Drain and pat dry with paper towels.
3. Pour red wine vinegar over the meat and add garlic. In a small bowl, combine salt, garlic powder, cinnamon, rosemary, Italian seasoning and pepper. Rub over the meat. Add oil and rub again.
4. In a small bowl, combine Tamarind Chutney and barbecue sauce. Transfer lamb shanks to the pan and pour half of the sauce over the meat. Cover with foil and bake in the oven for 1 1/2 hours. Uncover, pour in remaining sauce and continue baking for 30 minutes more.

INGREDIENTS

4 lamb shanks
1 Tbsp (15 mL) white vinegar
1/2 cup (125 mL) red wine vinegar
1 Tbsp (15 mL) mince garlic
1 Tbsp (15 mL) fine sea salt
1 Tbsp (15 mL) garlic powder
1 Tbsp (15 mL) ground cinnamon
2 sprigs fresh rosemary leaves
1 Tbsp (15 mL) Italian seasoning
1 tsp (5 mL) freshly ground black pepper
1/4 cup (60 mL) olive oil
2 cups (500 mL) Tamarind Chutney (see recipe, page 9)
1/4 cup (60 mL) sweet barbecue sauce

Bahama Rock Minced Lobster

I've titled this recipe "Bahama Rock" to pay homage to one of the greatest Bahamian musicians and folk artists, Mr. Ronnie Butler. His music and lyrics are inspiring, and embody the ethos of Bahamian culture, especially his popular song Bahama Rock.

Serves 6

1. In a 6-quart (6 L) pot with water, boil lobster tails over high heat for 5 minutes. Remove from the pot and let cool.
2. Using clean shears, remove lobster meat from the shells. Discard shells and place meat on a cutting board. Shred meat with a sharp knife or fork to pull the meat apart. Transfer to a large bowl. Add juice and seafood seasoning. Set aside.
3. In a large skillet, heat oil over medium heat. Add onion, garlic and green and red peppers and cook for 3 minutes.
4. Stir in tomato paste. Add tomato and cook for 2 minutes. Stir in stock and bring to a boil. Add lobster and remaining ingredients. Reduce heat and simmer, stirring occasionally, for 10 minutes. Adjust seasoning and serve at once over Steamed Coconut Jasmine Rice.

INGREDIENTS

6 Rock lobster tails (each about
   1 lb/450 g)
Juice of 2 lemons
2 Tbsp (30 mL) seafood seasoning
1/4 cup (60 mL) olive oil
1/2 large onion, diced
4 cloves garlic, diced
1/2 green bell pepper, diced
1/2 red bell pepper, diced
2 tsp (10 mL) tomato paste
1 ripe tomato, diced
1 cup (250 mL) water or fish stock
2 Tbsp (30 mL) Worcestershire sauce
3 sprigs fresh thyme leaves
1/4 tsp (1 mL) freshly ground
   black pepper
1 Tbsp (15 mL) Bahamian pepper sauce
   (see recipe page 3)
1 Tbsp (15 mL) diced fresh Italian Parsley
Steamed Coconut Jasmine Rice (see
   recipe, page 181)

EXUMA CRACKED CONCH

Here's an irresistible dish of tender conch meat breaded and deep fried in a crispy golden batter, reminiscent of the way it's prepared in Exuma. Serve it with Sweet Peppery Tartar Sauce (see recipe, page 5), Peas & Rice (see recipe, page 178) and Exotic Coleslaw (see recipe, page 120). The preparation of conch is a labor of love, as the slow boiling process for tender conch meat is about 1 hour. However, you may shorten the tenderizing time to 20 minutes in a pressure cooker.

Serves 4

1. Preheat a deep fryer with oil to 350°F (180°C).
2. In a large bowl, place conchs and season with 2 Tbsp (30 mL) of the seasoned salt. Set aside.
3. In another large bowl, whisk together buttermilk, eggs and remaining salt. Add flour to form a smooth batter.
4. Transfer seasoned conch meat to the buttermilk mixture. Place bread crumbs in a tray or pan. Remove conchs from the buttermilk mixture, letting excess drain off so the bread crumb coating will be even.
5. Remove conchs, one piece at a time, from the buttermilk mixture and dip in the bread crumbs. Cover with crumbs and press gently, making sure it's coated completely. Remove and shake off excess.
6. Place meat in the basket of the deep fryer and fry until golden. Set aside on a cooling rack placed over a sheet pan and keep warm. Repeat with the other meat.
7. Serve at once with lime wedges.

TIP: For a delicious snack, serve with GoomBay Sauce (see recipe, page 5) and hand-cut fries.

INGREDIENTS

Canola or vegetable oil

2 1/2 lbs (1.1 kg) Queen conchs, tenderized and cut into 4 pieces (see method, page 18)

1/4 cup (60 mL) Raquel's Seasoned Salt (see recipe, page 2), divided

2 1/4 cups (560 mL) buttermilk

2 eggs, lightly beaten

2 cups (500 mL) all-purpose flour

1 1/2 cups (375 mL) plain or panko bread crumbs

2 limes, cut into wedges

ABACO STEAMED CONCH

I've found that most people who have never cooked conch before assume that they could just "fire up the grill" and barbecue this mollusk. Unfortunately, this method would never work, as conch meat must be tenderized before the cooking process. Steaming is the perfect method for achieving delectable melt-in-your-mouth savory conch.

Serves 4

1. In a large bowl, place conchs and season with seasoned salt. Set aside.
2. In a 6-quart (6 L) pot , heat oil over medium heat. Add onion, garlic, bell pepper and potato and cook for 3 minutes. Add tomatoes and cook for 3 minutes.
3. Stir in ketchup and reserved stock and bring to a boil. Add conch and remaining ingredients. Reduce heat and simmer, covered with a lid that is slightly ajar, for 45 minutes. Adjust seasoning. Add a little warm water if the gravy is too thick (should coat the back of a spoon). Serve over peas and grits.

INGREDIENTS

2 Queen conchs, tenderized and cut into 1-inch (2.5 cm) segments (see method, page 18)
3 Tbsp (45 mL) Raquel's Seasoned Salt (see recipe, page 2)
3 Tbsp (45 mL) olive oil
1/2 large sweet onion, thinly sliced
4 cloves garlic, diced
1/2 green bell pepper, diced
1 large Caribbean sweet potato, diced
1 cup (250 mL) diced tomatoes
1/2 cup (125 mL) ketchup
3 cups (750 mL) reserved conch stock
3 Tbsp (45 mL) Worcestershire sauce
1 Tbsp (15 mL) molasses
3 sprigs fresh thyme leaves
1 Scotch bonnet pepper, diced
1 Tbsp (15 mL) diced fresh Italian parsley
Rum Cay Peas & Grits (omit conch) (see recipe, page 179)

Nassau Grouper Fingers

Grouper meat is lean and succulent with large flakes and a firm texture. The Nassau grouper is the national fish of The Bahamas. Grouper is related to the sea bass family so there's a variety available at your local fishmonger. It's imperative not to overcook this meaty and delicate fish, as the meat will become dry and chewy. Serve with Sweet Peppery Tartar Sauce, Peas & Rice with Coconut Oil and Twice-Fried plantains (see recipes, pages 5 and 178 and 109).
Serves 4

1. Preheat a deep fryer with oil to 350°F (180°C).
2. Rinse fillets in a bowl of salted water and pat dry with paper towels.
3. Transfer fish to a cutting board and season both sides with fish seasoning. Squeeze lime juice over the fillets and set aside.
4. In a large bowl, whisk together the buttermilk and eggs. Add 2 1/4 cups (560 mL) flour to form a smooth batter.
5. Transfer seasoned fish to the buttermilk mixture. In a large food storage bag, add remaining 4 cups (1 L) flour and black pepper. Set aside.
6. Remove fish, 3 pieces at a time, from buttermilk mixture, place in the flour mixture and shake to coat.
7. Place fish in the basket of the deep fryer and fry until golden, about 5–10 minutes. Set aside on a cooling rack placed over a baking sheet lined with parchment and keep warm. Repeat with the other fish.
8. Serve at once with lime wedges.

INGREDIENTS

Canola or vegetable oil
2 lbs (1 kg) grouper fillet, cut into 1-inch (2.5 cm) thick strips
Juice of 2 limes
2 Tbsp (30 mL) Bahama Fish Seasoning (see recipe, page 2)
2 cups (500 mL) buttermilk
2 eggs, lightly beaten
2 1/4 cups (560 mL) + 4 cups (1 L) all-purpose flour, divided
2 tsp (10 mL) freshly ground black pepper
2 limes, cut into wedges

BAHAMA GRILLED GROUPER IN PARCHMENT

This delightful dish of grouper is sealed in parchment paper then wrapped in foil and cooked on the grill in citrus and its own juices for a robust flavor. In France, this process is called en papillote; Italians call it al cartoccio, and in The Bahamas we call it "cooking in foil."

Serves 4

1. Fire up the grill to medium heat.
2. Rinse fillets in a bowl of salted water and pat dry with paper towels.
3. Transfer fish to a cutting board and season with seafood seasoning.
4. In a large skillet, heat oil over medium-high heat. Add onion, green and red peppers and potato and sauté, stirring, for 5 minutes. Season with salt to taste. Remove from heat and set aside.
5. Tear 4 sheets of foil and parchment paper large enough to fold over the fish. Place a piece of parchment paper over the foil, then place fish in the center. Divide and place the remaining ingredients equally over each fish (except lime and orange juices and pepper sauce). Season with salt and pepper.
6. Fold the papers towards the fish to form a pocket. In a small bowl, combine lime and orange juices and pepper sauce and evenly pour over the packets of fish. Continue to fold the papers over the fish to seal together tightly (making sure no steam escapes).
7. Place the foil parcels over indirect heat and grill for 30 minutes. Serve at once.

INGREDIENTS

4 thick grouper fillets, cut into 5-inch (12 cm) pieces

1/4 cup (60 mL) Bahama Fish Seasoning (see recipe, page 2)

1 large sweet onion, sliced

1/2 green bell pepper, sliced

1/2 red bell pepper, sliced

1 large sweet potato, diced

Salt and pepper to taste

2 plantains, ripe but firm, sliced 1/2-inch (1 cm) thick on the diagonal

2 cups (500 mL) sliced colorful cherry tomatoes

4 sprigs fresh thyme

Pepper to taste

1 cup (250 mL) fresh lime juice

1 cup (250 mL) fresh orange juice

1/2 cup (125 mL) Bahamian Pepper Sauce (see recipe, page 3)

EARTHY MOROS (CUBAN RICE & BEANS)

Cuban food is very soulful and vibrant, which is why I enjoy it immensely. We use practically the same spices and bold flavors so our food is never bland. I love a good fusion, so pair this aromatic rice with steamed chicken or pork.

Serves 6–8

1. Rinse beans in a medium bowl with water and remove any small stones.
2. In a 6-quart (6 L) Dutch oven, combine beans and ham hock, cover with water and bring to a boil over high heat.
3. Add onion, garlic, serrano pepper, bay leaf, thyme, cumin and cayenne pepper. Reduce heat and simmer, covered with the lid slightly ajar, for 1 1/2 hours, checking occasionally to replenish the water to cover.
4. Meanwhile, rinse rice in a medium bowl covered with water. Drain and set aside.
5. Add bell pepper and vinegar to the beans. Adjust seasoning and cook for 15 minutes more.
6. Remove ham and shred or cut into bite-size pieces. Discard the bone and set the meat aside. Remove and discard bay leaf, thyme sprigs and serrano pepper. Mash some of the beans in the pot with a masher. Remove from heat.
7. In a 3-quart (3 L) pot, heat oil over medium-high heat. Add rice and toast, stirring, for 2 minutes.
8. Stir in 2 cups (500 mL) of the beans to the rice with enough liquid to cover the rice by 1/2 inch (1 cm) (add hot water to beans if there's not enough of the bean liquid to cover rice). Place ham over rice. Reduce heat to the lowest setting and cook, covered tightly, for 15 minutes.
9. Fluff rice with a fork and serve at once.

TIP: Store remaining black beans in a large freezer bag for up to 1 month. Thaw beans and use for soup, salsa and rice recipes.

INGREDIENTS

3 cups (750 mL) small dried black beans
1 lb (450 kg) ham hock
1 medium Spanish onion, diced
4 cloves garlic, sliced
1 serrano pepper
1 bay leaf
3 sprigs fresh thyme leaves
1 tsp (5 mL) ground cumin
1 tsp (5 mL) cayenne pepper
4 cups (1 L) uncooked jasmine rice
1/2 red bell pepper
1/4 cup (60 mL) balsamic vinegar
Sea salt and pepper to taste
3 Tbsp (45 mL) olive oil

RICE & PEAS

The difference between Jamaica's Rice & Peas and The Bahamas'
Peas & Rice is mainly about the ratio of peas (or beans) to rice. Rice
& Peas is a vegetarian dish, whereas Peas & Rice is usually flavored
with salted beef. The flavors are distinctive but rest assured that
they're both exceptional rice dishes.

Serves 6–8

1. Rinse rice in a medium bowl covered with water. Drain and
   set aside.
2. In a 3-quart (3 L) pot, combine beans and garlic and enough
   water to cover over medium-high heat. Bring to a boil.
   Reduce heat and simmer for 45 minutes (add the coconut
   milk after 30 minutes) or until beans are cooked when
   pierced with a fork.
3. Add browning, salt, sugar, allspice, green onions, thyme and
   green and red bell peppers and cook 15 minutes more.
4. Stir in rice and 1/2 cup (125 mL) hot water to cover. Reduce
   heat to the lowest setting. Add Scotch bonnet pepper and
   cook, about 15 minutes.
5. Fluff with a fork and serve at once.

INGREDIENTS

4 cups (1 L) uncooked long-grain rice
1 cup (250 mL) dried red kidney beans,
   pre-soaked overnight
4 cloves garlic, smashed and diced
2 cups (500 mL) coconut milk
1 tsp (5 mL) browning (see page 219)
1 1/2 tsp (7 mL) salt
2 tsp (10 mL) brown sugar
1 Tbsp (15 mL) allspice berries, cracked
2 green onions, thinly sliced
   on the diagonal
1 tsp (5 mL) fresh thyme leaves
1/4 green bell pepper, diced
1/4 red bell pepper, diced
1/2 cup (125 mL) hot water
1 whole green Scotch bonnet pepper

Diri ak Djon-Djon (Rice with Mushrooms)

Djon-Djon are tiny mushrooms with a wonderful pungent flavor that are unique to Haiti. Their distinctive dark-smoky color are the foundation for this fragrant rice. Djon-djon are available in maggi bouillon cubes or the actual dried mushrooms at Haitian markets.

Serves 6

1. In a 3-quart (3 L) saucepan with 3 cups (750 mL) of water, add bouillon cubes over medium heat and bring to a boil. Reduce heat and simmer until cubes dissolve. Set aside.

2. In a medium bowl, cover rice with water and rinse. Drain and set aside.

3. In a 3-quart (3 L) pot, heat oil over medium-high heat. Add garlic and cook for 1 minute. Add rice and toast, stirring, for 2 minutes. Season with salt.

4. Pour in boiling water to cover the rice by 1/2 inch (1 cm). Add conchs over rice. Add parsley and thyme. Reduce heat to the lowest setting and cook rice, covered, for 15 minutes. Fluff with a fork and serve at once.

TIP: Conch may be substituted with seafood of your choice. Make a one-pot dish by adding a combination of seafood (shrimp, lobster, crab, scallops, etc.)

INGREDIENTS

2 djon-djon bouillon cubes (concentrated mushrooms)
4 cups (1 L) uncooked white long-grain rice
3 Tbsp (45 mL) olive oil
4 garlic cloves, sliced
2 tsp (10 mL) fine sea salt
Boiling water
2 Queen conchs, tenderized and cut into 1-inch (2.5 cm) segments (see method, page 18)
3 sprigs Italian parsley
3 sprigs fresh thyme

PEAS & RICE WITH COCONUT OIL

Bahamians take great pride in their national rice dish (Peas and Rice). We compare each other's rice with our grandmother's recipe, we take note of whether it was cooked with pigeon peas, sand peas or green peas, we identify what shade of brown is the most enticing, and we consider whether it is better to add flavor to the rice with salted beef or smoked ham. Whatever the case might be, we appreciate our heritage.

Serves 6

1. Rinse peas in a medium bowl with water and remove any small stones.
2. In a 6-quart (6 L) Dutch oven, combine peas and beef, cover with water and bring to a boil over high heat. Add celery, bay leaf and garlic. Reduce heat and simmer for 1 hour.
3. Remove and discard celery and bay leaf. Drain and reserve the stock and set aside the peas.
4. In a 3-quart (3 L) pot, heat oil over medium heat. Add onion and garlic and cook for 2 minutes. Add paste and cook, stirring, for 1 minute.
5. Add hot stock and bring to a boil. Add browning, seasoned salt, pepper, thyme and milk powder and stir.
6. Stir in rice. Add peas, beef and parsley. Reduce heat to the lowest setting and cook rice, covered, for 15 minutes or until the water evaporates.
7. Fluff with a fork and serve at once.

TIP: If the rice is too grainy, sprinkle with water and cover tightly with foil, then cover with the lid. Continue to cook the rice on low for 5 minutes more.

INGREDIENTS

2 cups (500 mL) dried pigeon peas

1 lb (450 g) salted beef, bone-in, cut into 1-inch (2.5 cm) pieces

1 stalk celery, cut in half widthwise

1 bay leaf

4 cloves garlic, peeled, smashed and sliced

1/2 cup (125 mL) coconut oil

1/2 onion, diced

4 cloves garlic, diced

1 Tbsp (15 mL) tomato paste

2 1/2 cups (625 mL) reserved stock

1 Tbsp (15 mL) browning (see page 219)

1 Tbsp (15 mL) Raquel's Seasoned Salt (see recipe, page 2)

1/4 tsp (1 mL) freshly ground black pepper

2 tsp (10 mL) fresh thyme leaves

1/4 cup (60 mL) coconut milk powder

4 cups (1 L) uncooked long-grain rice

3 sprigs Italian parsley

Salt to taste

Rum Cay Peas & Grits with Conch

Creamy grits are versatile and can be consumed for breakfast, lunch or dinner. In The Bahamas, we prepare the white or native yellow corn grits for breakfast or lunch, and for dinner we add meat or seafood and tint the grits with browning. In the past, grits were known as peasant comfort food; however, in modern times, grits and polenta are available on menus at fine-dining restaurants.

Serves 8

1. In a 4-quart (4 L) pot, heat oil over medium heat. Add onion, garlic and bell pepper and cook for 3 minutes.
2. Add paste, tomatoes and thyme and cook, stirring, for 3 minutes more. Stir in reserved conch stock, boiling water, browning, salt and pepper and bring to a boil.
3. Remove pot from heat and pour in grits, stirring with a wooden spoon (this prevents the grits from clumping together). Return pot to heat and reduce to the lowest setting.
4. Add peas and conch, cover with a lid that is slightly ajar, and cook, about 5–10 minutes. Serve at once.

INGREDIENTS

1/4 cup (60 mL) olive oil

1/2 medium onion, finely diced

2 garlic cloves, finely diced

1/4 piece green bell pepper, diced

1 tsp (5 mL) tomato paste

1/2 cup (125 mL) diced ripe tomatoes

2 tsp (10 mL) fresh thyme leaves

4 cups (1 L) reserved conch stock, heated

4 cups (1 L) boiling water

1 Tbsp (15 mL) browning (see page, 219)

1 1/2 tsp (7 mL) salt

1/4 tsp (1 mL) freshly ground black pepper

2 cups (500 mL) white grits

1/2 cup (125 mL) canned pigeon peas, rinsed

2 Queen conchs, tenderized and cut into 1/2-inch (1 cm) pieces (see method, page 18)

Curried Rice

This rice is filled with fragrant and elusive flavors and is great for pairing with poultry, and roast or braised meats.

Serves 6

1. In a medium bowl, cover rice with water and rinse. Drain and set aside.
2. In a 3-quart (3 L) pot, heat oil over medium heat. Add curry powder and cook for 3 minutes or until fragrant. Add cumin, cardamom, onion, garlic, ginger and thyme and cook for 2 minutes more.
3. Add rice and cook, stirring, for 1 minute. Increase heat to high. Add hot stock to cover. Stir in allspice, turmeric and sea salt. Bring to a boil. Reduce heat to the lowest setting and cook, covered, for 8 minutes or until water evaporates and rice is cooked (not grainy). Fluff with a fork and serve at once.

INGREDIENTS

4 cups (1 L) uncooked jasmine or long-grain rice
3 Tbsp (45 mL) canola oil
1 Tbsp (15 mL) Caribbean curry powder
1 tsp (5 mL) ground cumin
1 tsp (5 mL) ground cardamom
1/2 medium onion, diced
4 garlic cloves, diced
1 tsp (5 mL) minced ginger
2 tsp (10 mL) chopped fresh thyme
2 1/2 cups (625 mL) chicken stock, heated
1 tsp (5 mL) ground allspice berries
1 tsp (5 mL) ground turmeric
2 tsp (10 mL) fine sea salt

Steamed Coconut Jasmine Rice

Your family and friends will crave a second helping of this aromatic and nutty rice.

Serves 6

1. In a medium bowl, cover rice with water and rinse. Drain and set aside.
2. In a 3-quart (3 L) pot, heat oil over medium heat. Add garlic and ginger and cook for 1 minute.
3. Increase heat to high. Stir in rice and salt and toast for 2 minutes. Stir in boiling water, milk powder and sugar. Reduce heat to the lowest setting. Cook rice, covered, for 15 minutes or until water evaporates.
4. Fluff with a fork and serve at once.

INGREDIENTS

4 cups (1 L) uncooked jasmine rice
3 Tbsp (45 mL) coconut oil
2 cloves garlic, diced
2 tsp (10 mL) minced ginger
1 1/2 tsp (7 mL) salt
2 1/2 cups (625 mL) boiling hot water
1 cup (250 mL) coconut milk powder
1 Tbsp (15 mL) light brown sugar

Mad Mac & Cheese

Bahamian mac and cheese (aka macaroni) is the most rich, luscious and cheesy baked dish. Every family takes pride in their recipe. However, my girlfriend, Maddie, makes the most illustrious macaroni in the Bahamas. I've added a few ingredients to put my spin on it.

Serves 10

1. Preheat oven to 375˚F (190˚C). Set aside a 13- x 9-inch (33 x 23 cm) baking dish.
2. Fill a 4-quart (4 L) wide-bottomed pot halfway filled with water, and stir in oil, onion, celery, bell pepper and pasta over medium-high heat until al dente, about 8 minutes.
3. Drain pasta in a colander and transfer to a large bowl.
4. Add butter and mix to coat pasta. Add evaporated and whole milk, half of the marbled cheddar and Parmigiano-Reggiano and mix.
5. Add cream, eggs, seasoned salt, thyme, hot sauce, 1 cup (250 mL) cheddar (reserving remaining cheddar for the topping) and sour cream and mix again.
6. Adjust seasoning, then transfer mixture to the baking dish. Top with remaining cheese and sprinkle with paprika. Bake for about 30 minutes.
7. Remove macaroni from the oven and let set for 10 minutes. Cut into squares and serve at once.

INGREDIENTS

3 Tbsp (45 mL) olive oil

1/2 medium sweet onion, finely diced

2 stalks celery, finely diced

1/2 red bell pepper, finely diced

4 cups (1 L) elbow pasta

2 Tbsp (30 mL) butter

2 cups (500 mL) evaporated milk

1 cup (250 mL) whole milk

5 cups (1.25 L) shredded marbled cheddar cheese, divided

1 cup (250 mL) Parmigiano-Reggiano

4 cups (1 L) whipping (or heavy) cream (35%)

2 eggs, lightly beaten

2 Tbsp (30 mL) Raquel's Seasoned Salt (see recipe, page 2)

2 tsp (10 mL) fresh thyme leaves

1 Tbsp (15 mL) Caribbean hot sauce

1 1/2 cups (375 mL) sour cream

1 tsp (5 mL) paprika

Salt and pepper to taste

SWEET POTATO MASH

The holidays would not be the same if I didn't include my never-to-be-forgotten sweet mashed potatoes made with a combination of Caribbean Sweet potatoes and yellow-fleshed potatoes.
Serves 6

1. Separate potatoes into two 3-quart (3 L) pots filled with cold water (their different textures mean that one cooks faster than the next). Place over medium heat and bring to a boil and cook until tender when pierced with a paring knife, 15 minutes for yellow-fleshed potatoes and 30 minutes for Caribbean potatoes.
2. In a large bowl, mash potatoes together with a ricer or potato masher.
3. In a small 1-quart (1 L) saucepan, combine cream and butter over medium heat and cook until cream thickens slightly or forms tiny bubbles.
4. Add cheese and season to taste with salt and pepper.
5. Remove pan from heat. Mix in mashed potatoes and combine thoroughly. Fold in parsley and serve at once.

INGREDIENTS

4 large Caribbean sweet potatoes, peeled and cut into 1-inch (2.5 cm) pieces
2 yellow-fleshed potatoes, peeled and cut into 1-inch (2.5 cm) pieces
1 cup (250 mL) whipping (or heavy) cream (35%)
1 Tbsp (15 mL) butter
1/4 cup (60 mL) Parmigiano-Reggiano
Salt and white pepper to taste
1 Tbsp (15 mL) diced fresh Italian parsley

ROASTED SAGE & GARLIC MASHED CASSAVAS

Cassavas are long and tapered with shiny brown skin. Their edible starchy tuberous roots can be prepared like potatoes. In this dish, it's a tasty alternative to mashed potatoes.

Serves 4

1. Preheat oven to 375°F (190°C).
2. Cut 1/4-inch (6 mm) off the top off the head of garlic to expose the cloves and discard. Place garlic in the center of a foil sheet. Sprinkle salt and pepper over the cloves and drizzle with 1 Tbsp (15 mL) olive oil. Fold foil to seal securely. Place in a small ovenproof dish and roast for 30 minutes. Set aside and let cool.
3. In a small skillet, heat remaining oil over medium heat. Add sage leaves and fry until crisp, about 1 minute. Transfer to paper towels to drain. Crush the leaves in a small dish and set aside.
4. In a 4-quart (4 L) pot, place cassavas and cover with cold salted water over high heat. Bring to a boil. Reduce heat to medium and cook cassavas, about 30 minutes or until tender when pierced with a paring knife. Drain. Transfer to a large bowl and mash. Mash garlic and fold into mashed cassavas.
5. In a small 1-quart (1 L) saucepan, add cream and butter over medium heat and cook, stirring, until cream thickens slightly or forms tiny bubbles. Add cheese and season to taste with salt and pepper. Remove pan from heat. Pour over cassavas and mix thoroughly. Serve at once.

INGREDIENTS

1 head garlic
Salt and white pepper to taste
1/2 cup (125 mL) olive oil, divided
1/2 bunch fresh sage leaves
4 cassavas, peeled and cut into 1-inch (2.5 cm) pieces
1 1/2 cups (375 mL) whipping (or heavy) cream (35%)
2 Tbsp (30 mL) butter
1/4 cup (60 mL) Parmigiano-Reggiano

FENNEL SPICED CABBAGE

Here's a salutary and delightful accompaniment to meats, seafood and rice.

Serves 6

1. In a large skillet, heat oil and butter over medium heat.
2. Add garlic and bell pepper and cook for 2 minutes. Add green and red cabbages, in batches, and cook until slightly wilted, about 5–10 minutes.
3. Add remaining ingredients and cook for 3 minutes more. Serve at once.

INGREDIENTS

3 Tbsp (45 mL) olive oil
1 Tbsp (15 mL) butter
2 cloves garlic, diced
1/2 red bell pepper, thinly sliced
1/2 head savoy or green cabbage, shredded
1/4 piece red cabbage, shredded
1 medium carrot, julienned
Juice of 1 lemon
1 tsp (5 mL) dried Italian seasoning
1 Tbsp (15 mL) ground fennel
1/4 tsp (1 mL) smoked paprika
Salt and pepper to taste

Switcha Root Vegetables

Switcha is Bahamian jargon for limeade or lemonade. In the old days it was served in chilled mugs or glass jars. I'm revisiting my childhood memories with sweet roasted citrus-root vegetables.

Serves 8

1. Preheat oven to 400°F (200°C). Line a baking sheet with parchment paper and set aside.
2. In a small 1-quart (1 L) saucepan, add limeade, butter, mustard, honey and thyme over medium heat. Stir and bring to a boil. Let simmer for 5 minutes, then remove from the heat.
3. In a large bowl, combine red onions, garlic, cassava, sweet potatoes and carrots. Pour limeade mixture over the vegetables and toss. Sprinkle with salt and pepper. Transfer to the baking sheet and bake, about 45 minutes.
4. Garnish with lime zest and serve at once.

INGREDIENTS

2 cups (500 mL) frozen limeade concentrate, thawed
1/4 cup (60 mL) butter, melted
1 Tbsp (15 mL) whole-grain mustard
3 Tbsp (45 mL) honey
2 tsp (10 mL) fresh thyme leaves
2 medium red onions, quartered
1 head garlic, cloves peeled
1 cassava, peeled and cut into 1-inch (2.5 cm) pieces
1 sweet potato, peeled and cut into 1-inch (2.5 cm) pieces
1 Caribbean sweet potato, peeled and cut into 1-inch (2.5 cm) pieces (see page 223)
2 cups (500 mL) baby carrots
Salt and pepper to taste
Zest of 2 limes, for garnish

ROASTED CORN WITH MAPLE CHILE DRESSING

I believe that the love for roasted corn is universal…people tend to follow the signs that read "Fresh Roasted Corn!" Here's another extraordinary recipe to add to your repertoire.

Serves 6

1. Fire up the grill to medium-high. In a small bowl, combine mayonnaise, maple syrup and sambal oelek. Set aside.
2. Brush the cooked corn with olive oil and place on grill, turning occasionally, until corn is slightly charred all over, about 10-15 minutes.
3. Spread sauce evenly over corn. Top with cheese. Cover grill and melt cheese for 3-5 minutes. Garnish with parsley and serve at once.

INGREDIENTS

2 cups (500 mL) mayonnaise
1/4 cup (60 mL) pure maple syrup
1 Tbsp (15 mL) sambal oelek
6 ears corn, cooked (husk discarded)
Olive oil
1 1/2 cups (375 mL) shredded
    Parmigiano-Reggiano
1 Tbsp (15 mL) diced fresh
    Italian parsley

Sautéed Callaloo

Callaloo (also known as Chinese spinach) is the ultimate beneficial leafy green vegetable. It's the leaves from the taro root and it's similar in taste to creamy spinach, with a delightful nutty undertone. Fresh callaloo is high in calcium, iron, protein and fiber, and is readily available at Caribbean and Asian supermarkets.

Serves 4

1. In a 1-quart (1 L) saucepan, cover beef with water to cover over medium-high heat and bring to a boil. Reduce heat and simmer for 30 minutes. Let cool. Transfer to the bowl of a food processor to shred with 1/2 cup (125 mL) of the liquid and set aside.
2. Remove stalk and midrib from callaloo leaves. Rinse leaves under cold water and roughly tear.
3. Have a bowl of ice water handy. Fill a 4-quart (4L) pot halfway with water and heat over high heat; bring to a boil. Add leaves and boil until vibrant green, then blanch in the bowl of ice water to stop the cooking process. Squeeze the leaves to drain the water and set aside.
4. In a large skillet, heat ghee over medium heat. Add onion, garlic, ginger paste and chadon beni and cook, stirring, for 2 minutes.
5. Add callaloo leaves, in batches, and sauté, about 10 minutes. Add Scotch bonnet pepper (if using) and shredded beef. Season to taste. Add lemon juice and serve garnished with lemon zest.

INGREDIENTS

1 cup (250 mL) salted beef, boneless (optional)
1 bunch callaloo leaves
1/4 cup (60 mL) ghee
1/2 medium red onion, diced
4 cloves garlic, diced
1 tsp (5 mL) ginger paste
1 Tbsp (15 mL) diced chadon beni
1/4 Scotch bonnet pepper, finely diced (optional)
Salt and pepper to taste
Zest and juice of 1 lemon

BAKED BLACK-EYED PEAS

This appealing side dish is a wonderful accompaniment to barbecues and could be served hot or at room temperature.

Serves 8

1. Preheat oven to 350°F (180°C). Set aside a 13- x 9-inch (33 x 23 cm) baking dish.
2. Remove any stones from peas and soak overnight.
3. In a 4-quart Dutch oven, cover peas with water to cover over high heat; bring to a boil. Reduce heat; simmer and cook until peas are tender, about 45 minutes.
4. Drain peas in a colander and transfer to the baking dish. Add remaining ingredients (except parsley). Cover with foil and bake for 2 hours or until sauce is slightly thickened. Remove thyme sprigs and bay leaf. Garnish with parsley and serve at once.

INGREDIENTS

2 cups (500 mL) dried black-eyed peas
1 medium sweet onion, sliced and cut in half
4 cloves garlic, diced
1/2 green bell pepper, diced
3 Tbsp (45 mL) Worcestershire Sauce
3 cups (750 mL) diced stewed tomatoes
2 Tbsp (30 mL) molasses
2 cups (500 mL) vegetable or mushroom stock
3 sprigs fresh thyme
1 bay leaf
1 tsp (5 mL) ground cumin
1 tsp (5 mL) ground coriander
1 tsp (5 mL) ground cinnamon
1/2 tsp (2 mL) ground allspice berries
1 Tbsp (15 mL) Caribbean hot sauce
Salt and pepper to taste
2 Tbsp (30 mL) diced fresh Italian parsley

SPICED POPCORN CAULIFLOWER

Slightly sweet and nutty cauliflower is a tasty side dish and it's even better as a snack.

Serves 4

1. Preheat oven to 375°F (190°C). Line a baking sheet with parchment paper.
2. In a small dish, combine salt, cumin, fennel and cinnamon and mix. Melt ghee in the microwave.
3. In a large bowl, place cauliflower florets. Add melted ghee and spice mix and toss.
4. Transfer florets to the baking sheet. Adjust seasoning with salt and pepper and bake, for about 30 minutes or until tender. Garnish with paprika and parsley and serve at once.

INGREDIENTS

1 tsp (5 mL) salt
2 tsp (10 mL) ground cumin
2 tsp (10 mL) ground fennel
1/2 tsp (2 mL) ground cinnamon
1/2 cup (125 mL) ghee
Salt and white pepper to taste
1/4 tsp (1 mL) smoked paprika
1 Tbsp (15 mL) diced fresh
   Italian parsley
1 head cauliflower, florets cut in half

CHAPTER 6

SWEET *Endings*

- PETIT GUAVA DUFF

- BERRY ISLAND DUMPLINGS WITH
  BUTTERSCOTCH SAUCE

- COCONUT CUSTARD PIE

- TROPICAL MANGO CHEESECAKE
  WITH SEA GRAPE PEARLS

- ELEUTHERA PINEAPPLE TART WITH
  PISTACHIO BUTTER

- EXOTIC SOUFFLÉS

- CHOCOLATE COCONUT PURSES WITH
  BANANA CARAMEL

- AUNT TIA'S COCONUT CREAM BARS

- CARIBBEAN BREAD PUDDING WITH
  GINGER-COOKED CREAM

- SAPODILLA-SPICED CAKE WITH
  DILLY CREAM

Petit Guava Duff

Guava duff is the national dessert of The Bahamas and rightfully so—it's an extraordinary dessert of delectable guavas nestled in a roulade and generously drizzled with a guava rum sauce.

Serves 6

1. To prepare the dough, in the bowl of a stand mixer fitted with the paddle attachment, add flour, baking powder, sugar and salt. With the mixer on its lowest speed, mix in butter. Gradually pour in water and continue mixing until the dough comes together.
2. Dust a clean surface with flour, knead dough and form into a ball. Let rest for 10 minutes.
3. Roll dough out into a rectangular shape. Using a pastry cutter, divide dough into 3 roulades. Place sliced guavas over each dough, leaving about 1/2-inch (1 cm) border at the ends.
4. Roll dough into a 2-to 3-inch (5–8 cm) roulade, fold and seal both ends firmly by pinching together.
5. Tear a large enough piece of heavy-duty foil. Carefully transfer the roulade to one end of the foil, then roll loosely, allowing a little space for the dough to expand. Secure tightly by folding both ends upwards (this prevents water from entering during the steaming process). Repeat with the remaining dough.
6. Place the roulades over the rack of a 10-quart (10 L) oval roaster. Add a little water to reach 1 inch (2.5 cm) just below the rack. Place over high heat and bring to a boil, then cover tightly with a lid. Reduce heat and steam for 30 minutes, while replenishing the water level occasionally.

continued on page 196

INGREDIENTS

Dough
2 cups (500 mL) all-purpose flour
2 Tbsp (30 mL) baking powder
1/2 cup (125 mL) granulated sugar
1/4 tsp (1 mL) salt
2 Tbsp (30 mL) unsalted butter
2/3 cup (160 mL) water

1 cup (250 mL) pink guava shells, sliced

Rum Sauce
1/2 cup (125 mL) diced pink
  guava shells
1 cup (250 mL) whipping (or heavy)
  cream (35%)
1 cup (250 mL) condensed milk
1/2 cup (125 mL) evaporated milk
1 Tbsp (15 mL) pure vanilla extract
1/2 tsp (2 mL) ground nutmeg
1/2 cup (125 mL) granulated sugar
1/3 cup (80 mL) dark or spiced rum

Guava Crème
3 cups (750 mL) whipping (or heavy)
  cream (35%)
1/2 cup (125 mL) diced pink
  guava shells

1/4 cup (60 mL) whole mint leaves

7. Meanwhile, to prepare the rum sauce, in a blender, combine 1/2 cup (125 mL) diced guavas, cream, condensed milk, evaporated milk, vanilla, nutmeg, sugar and rum and purée.

8. To prepare the guava crème, in a bowl, whisk cream to stiff peaks. Fold in diced guavas. Cover with plastic and keep in the refrigerator until ready to use.

9. Carefully remove the roulade from the pan (as hot steam will escape). Remove and discard the foil. Place guava duffs on a platter and slice them into 2-inch (5 cm) thick pieces on the diagonal. Pour rum sauce over and serve garnished with guava crème and mint leaves.

CARIBBEAN BREAD PUDDING WITH GINGER-COOKED CREAM

Here's a dessert that makes you feel at home. I'm talking about that warm blissful feeling you experience every time you take a bite. All that's missing is a good cup of coffee.

Serves 10

1. Preheat oven to 375°F (190°C). Grease a 13- x 9-inch (33 x 23 cm) baking dish with butter. Sprinkle with flour, knocking off any excess; set aside.

2. In a large bowl, combine all ingredients (except sultanas and cooked cream) and, using a hand-held mixer on the first speed, mix well. Fold in sultanas.

3. Transfer mixture to baking pan and level with a spatula. Bake for about 50–60 minutes or until the center springs back when touched lightly. Serve warm in the center of a bowl with Ginger-Cooked Cream.

TIP: Top with an exotic mild-flavored ice cream (pineapple or coconut) and dehydrated ginger pieces.

INGREDIENTS

2 Tbsp (30 mL) butter
2 cups (500 mL) day-old bread
1 cup (250 mL) all-purpose flour
1/4 tsp (1 mL) salt
1 cup (250 mL) granulated sugar
2 tsp (10 mL) baking powder
1 large Caribbean sweet potato or Jamaican sweet potato, grated
5 cups (1.25 L) coconut milk
2 tsp (10 mL) pure vanilla extract
1/2 tsp (2 mL) ground nutmeg
Zest of 2 limes
1/3 cup (80 mL) white or spiced rum
1/2 cup (125 mL) golden sultanas (raisins)
3 cups (750 mL) Ginger-Cooked Cream (see recipe, page 13)

Coconut Custard Pie

Impress your family and friends with this simple but delectable dessert that will please even your most discerning guest. Serve with pistachio ice cream.

Makes two 9-inch (23 cm) pies

1. Preheat oven to 350°F (180°C).
2. Dock 2 store-bought or homemade pie crusts with a fork and bake for 5 minutes. Set aside.
3. In a large bowl using a hand-held mixer, combine all remaining ingredients and mix on the first speed setting for 2 minutes.
4. Pour filling into pie shells and bake, about 30–35 minutes or until set in the center.

INGREDIENTS

Two 9-inch (23 cm) store-bought pie crusts
2 cups (500 mL) frozen grated coconut, thawed
1 can (12 oz/354 mL) evaporated milk
1 can (14 oz/396 mL) condensed milk
1 cup (250 mL) granulated sugar
4 eggs, lightly beaten
3 Tbsp (45 mL) dark or spiced rum
2 tsp (10 mL) pure vanilla extract
2 tsp (10 mL) almond extract
1/4 tsp (1 mL) ground nutmeg

Tropical Mango Cheesecake with Sea Grape Pearls

Mango is hands-down my favorite fruit. With nuances of orange, peach and melon, it's like no other fruit. Ripe Kent, Palmer or any other type of non-fibrous mangoes are preferred for this bright and citrusy cheesecake.

Serves 8

1. Preheat oven to 300°F (150°C). Prepare a 10-inch (25 cm) springform pan by greasing the bottom and lining with a circle of parchment paper.
2. To prepare the crust, in a large bowl, combine graham cracker crumbs, brown sugar, lime zest, coconut and butter and mix until the crust is sandy and coarse.
3. Put the mixture into the lined springform pan. Press down with a spatula until it's compact. Bake for 10 minutes. Remove and let cool.
4. Increase oven temperature to 350°F (180°C).
5. To prepare the filling, in the bowl of a food processor, add mangoes and purée. Add remaining ingredients and purée until smooth.
6. Pour filling into crust in the pan, then place the pan on top of a baking sheet. Bake in the center of the oven, about 90 minutes or until set in the center. (To maintain a vibrant color, form a dome with a piece of foil over the pan).
7. Remove from oven. Let cool, then transfer to the refrigerator to chill for 1 hour.
8. Serve garnished with whipped cream, edible hibiscus and drizzle with syrup from the preserved hibiscus. Top with mint leaves and sea grape pearls.

TIP: Look for wild hibiscus in syrup at gourmet supermarkets.

INGREDIENTS

Crust
2 cups (500 mL) honey graham cracker crumbs
1/3 cup (80 mL) light brown sugar
2 tsp (10 mL) lime zest
1/4 cup (60 mL) coconut flakes, toasted
1 cup (250 mL) melted butter

Filling
4 ripe Kent mangoes, peeled and sliced
1 lb (450 g) cream cheese, softened
1 1/2 cups (375 mL) granulated sugar
1 vanilla bean pod
6 large eggs
Juice of 1 lemon

Garnish
Whipped cream
8 wild hibiscus in syrup
1 Tbsp (15 mL) mint leaves, chiffonade
1 cup (250 mL) Sea Grape Pearls (see recipe, page 14)

ELEUTHERA PINEAPPLE TART WITH PISTACHIO BUTTER

The most illustrious pineapples are found on the Island of Eleuthera, where every bakery has their family's version of pineapple tarts. There are tarts with a pineapple filling in a pie shell with lattice, or inside pastry dough as a turnover. I believe that it's the actual fruit and spiced filling that produces for the best pineapple tarts.

Serves 12

1. Preheat oven to 350°F (180°C). Grease a 9-inch (23 cm) pie pan with butter and sprinkle with flour. Set aside.
2. To prepare the pistachio butter, in the bowl of a food processor, combine pistachios, simple syrup and almond extract and purée until mixture forms a smooth paste. Set aside in a small dish.
3. To prepare the dough, follow recipe for johnny cake, omit coconut and add egg and mix. Dust a clean surface with flour. Cut dough in half and roll out both pieces to an 11-inch (28 cm) circle. Place 1 circle of dough over the pie pan, gently press down and along the sides to fit. Trim any additional dough hanging over the edge of the pan, then flute the edges with your fingers.
4. Roll over the remaining circle of dough with a lattice pie cutter, then gently pull to display the lattice design. Place over a plate lined with plastic wrap and set aside in the refrigerator.
5. To prepare the filling, in the bowl of a food processor, add pineapple and pulse a few times to crush.
6. Drain pineapple into a 3-quart (3 L) saucepan over medium heat. Stir in remaining ingredients and simmer for 10 minutes. Let cool.
7. Pour the filling into the pan, then flip the plate over with the lattice to cover and pinch the edges together. Brush with egg wash. Bake for 35 minutes. Let cool and serve with the Pistachio Butter.

INGREDIENTS

Pistachio Butter
2 1/2 cups (625 mL) shelled
   pistachios, toasted
3 Tbsp (45 mL) simple syrup
1 tsp (5 mL) almond extract

Dough
Aunt Tia's Johnny Cake (see recipe,
   page 34)
1 large egg, lightly beaten

Filling
2 cups (500 mL) diced fresh pineapple
1 cup (250 mL) simple syrup
1/2 tsp (2 mL) ground cinnamon
1/4 tsp (1 mL) grated nutmeg
1/4 tsp (1 mL) grated ground allspice

Egg wash

TIP: Simple syrup is available to purchase at supermarkets, however, you may make your own simple syrup by placing 1 part water to 1 part sugar in a 1-quart (1 L) saucepan over medium heat. Bring to a boil, reduce heat and simmer until mixture is bubbly and syrupy.

Exotic Soufflés

I couldn't have a chapter on desserts and exclude my all-time favorite. If soufflé is on the menu, that's what I'm having. Enlighten your palate with two of the most ambrosial fruits in these heavenly soufflés: mamey, which has the flavor of ripened apricots, and soursop, with its acidic-yet-mellow honeyed flavor, an epicurean delight!

Makes 10

1. Preheat oven to 375°F (190°C). Grease ten 8-oz (250 mL) ramekins with butter. Coat with sugar, knocking out any excess.
2. In the bowl of a stand mixer fitted with the paddle attachment, mix flour and butter together to form a smooth paste.
3. In a 1-quart (1 L) saucepan, combine 2/3 cup (160 mL) sugar and milk over medium heat and bring to a boil, stirring to dissolve the sugar. Remove from heat.
4. Using a wire whisk, vigorously beat in the flour paste, 1–2 Tbsp (15–30 mL) at a time to prevent any lumps. Return to heat and bring to a boil, beating constantly. Simmer for 5 minutes or until mixture is very thick. Transfer to a large bowl, cover and let cool for 10 minutes.
5. To prepare the grand mamey flavoring, in a bowl, combine all ingredients. Set aside.
6. To prepare the creamy soursop flavoring, in a bowl, combine all ingredients. Set aside.
7. In a small bowl, whisk egg yolks and vanilla together, then quickly beat into the flour paste mixture.
8. Beat egg whites until they form soft peaks. Add 1/3 cup (80 mL) sugar and continue beating until mixture forms firm, moist peaks (it should be stiff enough that if you turn the bowl over the mixture stays in place).
9. Fold egg whites into the soufflé base. Pour mixture into the prepared ramekins and smooth out the tops.
10. Place ramekins on a baking sheet and bake for 15 minutes. Serve at once with the Grand Mamey and Creamy Soursop flavorings on the side to spoon in the center of the soufflés.

INGREDIENTS

3/4 cup (190 mL) all-purpose flour
1/3 cup (80 mL) butter + extra
   for greasing
1 cup (250 mL) granulated sugar,
   divided + extra for coating
2 cups (500 mL) whole milk
Grand Mamey Flavoring (see below)
Creamy Soursop Flavoring (see below)
6 egg yolks
2 tsp (10 mL) pure vanilla extract
8 egg whites

Grand Mamey Flavoring

1 cup (250 mL) frozen mamey pulp or
   purée, thawed
1/4 cup (60 mL) condensed milk
3 Tbsp (45 mL) Grand Marnier

Creamy Soursop Flavoring

1 cup (250 mL) soursop nectar or juice
1/4 cup (60 mL) condensed milk
Pinch of nutmeg

Chocolate Coconut Purses with Banana Caramel

I would like to believe that this decadent dessert captures the essence of paradise.

Serves 8

1. Preheat oven to 375°F (190°C). Line food safe storage containers with wax paper and set aside.
2. To prepare the crème caramel, peel the label from can of condensed milk and place in the center of a 6-quart (6 L) pot. Cover with water by 1 inch (2.5 cm). Place pot over high heat and bring water to a boil. Reduce heat and simmer, about 2 hours (this can be done ahead of time), making sure to replenish the water. Let cool before opening.
3. To prepare the banana caramel, cut banana into 1-inch (2.5 cm) pieces and add to the bowl of a food processor. Add crème caramel and purée until smooth. Set aside.
4. To prepare the coconut truffles, in a 3-quart (3 L) saucepan, combine coconut, sugar and 1/4 cup (60 mL) of the evaporated milk over medium heat and stir occasionally until sugar dissolves and milk nearly evaporates. Reduce heat to low. In a small bowl, mix cornstarch and remaining 1/4 cup (60 mL) of evaporated milk. Stir into saucepan and let simmer for 5 minutes or until bubbly. Remove from heat.
5. Using a melon baller, scoop the coconut mixture into a ball and set aside on the wax paper.
6. Melt chocolate over a double broiler. Using a spoon, dip the coconut balls into the chocolate to coat one at a time, then return to the container lined with the wax paper. Transfer to the freezer and let set for 1 hour.

continued on page 208

continued on page 208

INGREDIENTS

Crème Caramel
1 can (14 oz/396 mL) condensed milk

Banana Caramel
1 ripe banana
1 cup (250 mL) reserved crème caramel

Coconut Truffles
2 cups (500 mL) grated coconut
1 1/2 cups (375 mL) granulated sugar
1/2 cup (125 mL) evaporated milk, divided
1 Tbsp (15 mL) cornstarch
1 tsp (5 mL) pure vanilla extract
1 tsp (5 mL) almond extract

2 cups (500 mL) semisweet chocolate, chopped
1 package phyllo pastry (thawed in the refrigerator)
1/2 cup (125 mL) butter, melted
Ice cream
Banana Caramel Sauce, for serving

7. Line a baking sheet with parchment paper. Lay 1 sheet of phyllo on a cutting board and brush with melted butter all over. Top with another sheet, smooth out and brush with butter again, then repeat with a third sheet. Using a paring knife, cut phyllo into 2-inch (5 cm) squares. Place a chocolate-coconut ball in the center of each square. Bring the edges together to form a parcel and pinch and twist gently to seal. Brush with butter again, then transfer to the baking sheet. Repeat with remaining coconut truffles. Wrap securely and return additional phyllo pastry to the freezer.

8. Bake for about 15 minutes or until phyllo is golden and chocolate melts. Serve 2–3 purses with a scoop of vanilla bean or black cherry ice cream drizzled with Banana-Caramel Sauce.

TIPS: Bake straight from the freezer to 400°F (200°C) preheated oven for 25–30 minutes.

To prepare the purses, phyllo pastry becomes dry and brittle very quickly, so as you work with it keep the unused portion covered with a piece of waxed paper.

AUNT TIA'S COCONUT CREAM BARS

This sentimental treat is from my childhood memories. It was my grandmother's reward system for being good. My Aunt Tia perfected this chewy and creamy treat. It was highly requested at school events and she continued the tradition of making them for my kids. The color can be pinkish or red and white. As an alternative to food coloring, I use vibrant and flavorful beet juice.

Makes sixteen 2-inch (5 cm) square bars

1. Fill a 1.5-quart (1.5 L) saucepan halfway with water. Add beet, bring to a boil over medium-high heat and cook until tender, about 30 minutes. Let cool.

2. Cut beet into quarters. Place half of the beets in the bowl of a food processor with the remaining water from the pan and purée. Set aside in a small dish.

3. In a 3-quart (3 L) saucepan, combine coconut, sugar, salt and water over medium-low heat and cook, stirring occasionally, until the water evaporates, about 30 minutes.

4. In an 8-inch (20 cm) square dish, place half of the coconut mixture and pack down with a spatula. This will form the bottom white portion of the bars.

5. Using a hand-held mixer, beat remaining coconut mixture to a fluff for 30 seconds. Add 3 Tbsp (45 mL) of the beet juice and stir to color evenly. Place over the coconut in the dish. Spread out and pack down lightly for both layers to adhere.

6. Cover dish with a cloth or paper towel and leave in a cool place to set for 8 hours. Cut into about sixteen 2-inch (5 cm) bars. Set on a plate and watch them quickly disappear.

INGREDIENTS

1 medium beet, peeled
2 cups (500 mL) frozen grated coconut, thawed
3 cups (750 mL) granulated sugar
1/4 tsp (1 mL) salt
1/2 cup (125 mL) water

Berry Island Dumplings with Butterscotch Sauce

As a child, I can recall a scrumptious dessert that my grandmother made on special occasions called Coconut Jimmy (coconut dumplings). It's the only recipe that I never took the time to learn, however, I still get lost in reverie thinking about the taste of those nostalgic dessert dumplings. I'm revisiting those memories in this recipe of homemade dumplings filled with a bold burst of berries, swimming in creamy butterscotch sauce.

Makes 24 dumplings

1. To prepare the butterscotch sauce, in a 1-quart (1 L) saucepan, combine the sugar and cream over medium heat and stir to dissolve sugar. Bring to a boil until tiny bubbles start to form, then remove from heat. Add butter and vanilla and stir until the butter melts. Set aside.
2. To prepare the dumplings, in a medium bowl, combine berries, lemon zest and juice and confectioner's sugar and toss without crushing the berries. Set aside.
3. In a large bowl, combine remaining dumpling ingredients and mix to form a dough. Knead a few times.
4. Dust a clean surface with flour. Using a rolling pin, roll the dough out into a 1/4-inch (6 mm) thick rectangle. Using a pastry cutter, cut about twenty 1 1/2- x 4-inch (4 x 10 cm) pieces of dough. Place 4 berries horizontally on each piece of dough. Wet the tips of your fingers, fold the dough over and seal by pinching the ends to make the berry-stuffed dumplings. Set on a plate lined with parchment paper and refrigerate for about 10–15 minutes.
5. Meanwhile, bring a 6-quart (6 L) pot with water over medium-high heat to a boil. Add dumplings, in batches of 6, and let cook, about 3–4 minutes. Remove with a slotted spoon, then transfer to a bowl. Repeat with remaining dumplings.
6. Pour butterscotch sauce over the dumplings. Garnish with sugar and serve with additional berries and Mint Crème.

INGREDIENTS

Butterscotch Sauce
1 1/2 cups (375 mL) light brown sugar
1 cup (250 mL) whipping (or heavy) cream (35%)
1/3 cup (80 mL) unsalted butter
1 Tbsp (15 mL) pure vanilla extract

Dumplings
1 cup (250 mL) blueberries
1 cup (250 mL) raspberries
Zest and juice of 1 lemon
2 Tbsp (30 mL) confectioner's (icing) sugar
2 cups (500 mL) all-purpose flour
1/3 cup (80 mL) granulated sugar
1/4 tsp (1 mL) salt
2 Tbsp (30 mL) coconut oil
2/3 cup (160 mL) water

Garnish
1/4 cup (60 mL) confectioner's (icing) sugar
1 cup (250 mL) mixed berries
2 cups (500 mL) Mint Crème (see recipe, page 4)

DINING IN PARADISE   211   SWEET ENDINGS

Sapodilla Spiced Cake with Dilly Cream

Sapodilla or dilly is another tasty fruit from my childhood memories. It has a mealy soft texture and a flavor like an over-ripe pear with nuances of brown sugar. Just pull the fruit apart when ripe and eat the soft and juicy flesh. It has become very popular in supermarkets, but you will always find them in Indian or Caribbean markets.
Serves 10

1. Preheat oven to 350°F (180°C). Grease a 10-cup (2.5 L) Bundt pan with butter. Dust with flour, knocking off any excess flour from the pan.
2. In the bowl of a stand mixer fitted with the paddle attachment, cream 1/2 cup (125 mL) butter with sugar.
3. In another large mixer bowl, sift dry ingredients together with the motor running on the first speed. Add to the creamed sugar, 1 cup (250 mL) at a time, until combined.
4. In a medium bowl, whisk together wet ingredients. With the motor running, add to flour mixture just until it forms a smooth batter, scraping down the sides with a spatula.
5. Pour batter over the pecans in the Bundt pan and level with a spatula. Transfer to the baking sheet and bake on the center rack, about 40 minutes until the top springs back and a toothpick inserted in the center comes out clean.
6. Let the cake cool in the pan, then hold a plate over the pan while flipping to release the cake.
7. To prepare the dilly cream, in a saucepan, add cream over medium heat and bring to a boil just until tiny bubbles start to form. Reduce heat. Add remaining ingredients and simmer for 3 minutes. Remove from heat. Let cool and pour half of the sauce over the Bundt, allowing it to drain down the sides for an enticing presentation.
8.

TIP Serve remaining sauce over vanilla ice cream, if desired.

INGREDIENTS

1 cup (250 mL) whole pecans
1/2 cup (125 mL) softened butter + extra for greasing
1 1/3 cups (330 mL) granulated sugar
2 cups (500 mL) all-purpose flour
2 tsp (10 mL) baking powder
1 cup (250 mL) vanilla powder
1 tsp (5 mL) ground cinnamon
1 tsp (5 mL) ground nutmeg
1/2 tsp (2 mL) ground cloves
1 tsp (5 mL) ground ginger
1/4 tsp (1 mL) salt
4 eggs
1 tsp (5 mL) pure vanilla extract
1 tsp (5 mL) almond extract
3 Tbsp (45 mL) canola oil
1 cup (250 mL) sapodilla purée
3/4 cup (190 mL) spiced rum
3/4 cup (190 mL) whole milk

Dilly Cream
1/2 cup (125 mL) whipping (or heavy) cream (35%)
1 cup (250 mL) condensed milk
1/4 cup (60 mL) sapodilla purée
1 tsp (5 mL) pure vanilla extract
1/4 cup (60 mL) Amaretto

CHAPTER 7

SAIL AWAY *Cocktails*

- SOURSOP PUNCH
- GOOMBAY SMASH
- YELLOW BIRD
- SKY JUICE
- VIVACIOUS SUNRISE

SOURSOP PUNCH

Here's a wonderful feel-so-good creamy cocktail. Who needs eggnog for the holidays!
Serves 8

1. Place all ingredients in a blender and mix well. Adjust to preferred consistency by adding additional water.
2. Serve over ice.

.

INGREDIENTS

1 cup (250 mL) soursop purée
   (see page 222)
2 cups (500 mL) water
1 cup (250 mL) evaporated milk
1 cup (250 mL) condensed milk
1/4 cup (60 mL) granulated sugar
Pinch of salt
1 tsp (5 mL) almond extract
1 tsp (5 mL) pure vanilla extract
1/4 tsp (1 mL) freshly grated nutmeg
1/3 cup (80 mL) dark rum
Ice

GOOMBAY SMASH

This is one of my favorite "take-me-away" island cocktails. It was first created in Green Turtle Cay, Abaco, by Ms. Emily Cooper, proprietor of the Blue Bee Bar.
Serves 2

1. Add all liquid ingredients to a cocktail shaker with ice. Shake well to chill.
2. Serve garnished with pineapple wedges and cherries.

INGREDIENTS

2 oz (60 mL) pineapple juice
2 oz (60 mL) orange juice
1 oz (30 mL) coconut rum
1/2 oz (15 mL) coconut cream
1/2 oz (15 mL) spiced rum
1/2 oz (15 mL) dark rum
Ice
2 pineapple wedges
2 cherries

Yellow Bird

This is the drink that was inspired by the popular song recorded by Harry Belafonte.

Serves 2

1. Add all ingredients to a shaker with ice. Shake well to chill.
2. Serve and garnish with orange slices and cherries.

INGREDIENTS

Juice of 1/2 lime
1 1/2 oz (45 mL) light rum
1/2 oz (15 mL) banana liqueur
1/2 oz (15 mL) Galliano liqueur
2 oz (60 mL) orange juice
2 oz (60 mL) pineapple juice
2 orange slices
2 cherries
Ice

Sky Juice

The incomparable sky juice is also known as "gully wash" or just "gin and coconut water" (attributed to the song by the Baha Men). For an island experience, chill and funnel this cocktail into empty coconut shells then serve it with straws. But take it easy. This one "sneaks up on you."

Serves 4

1. Place all ingredients in an empty 4-cup (1 L) bottle with a cover and shake well.
2. Refrigerate until very cold, about 2 hours.
3. Serve in chilled glasses or over ice or inside coconut shells.

INGREDIENTS

48 oz (1.36 L) coconut water
2 cups (500 mL) condensed milk
1/2 cup (125 mL) granulated sugar (optional)
1/2 cup (125 mL) diced coconut jelly
10 oz (300 mL) gin
1/4 tsp (1 mL) freshly grated nutmeg
Ice or coconut shells , for serving

Vivacious Sunrise

I adore this cocktail, especially since it was created by my significant other in my honor. I'm vivacious and I know it!

Makes 2 glasses

1. Place hibiscus in glasses.
2. Add all ingredients to a cocktail shaker with ice. Shake well and pour in glasses over the edible flowers to enjoy a sunny cocktail.

INGREDIENTS

2 wild hibiscus in syrup

10 oz (300 mL) sparkling lemonade, chilled

4 oz (110 mL) orange juice, chilled

4 oz (110 mL) pineapple juice, chilled

1 oz (30 mL) coconut rum

Ice

4 oz (110 mL) spiced rum

2 oz (60 mL) Grand Marnier

GLOSS*ary*

"We are more alike, my friends,
than we are unalike."
— Maya Angelou.

I think of this quote whenever I travel to different countries, sampling the food and immersing myself in the culture. Then I reflect on our similarities and appreciate the differences by embracing new experiences with an open mind. It's my hope that my readers will sample new ingredients and recipes with an open mind.

ALLSPICE BERRIES: This whole spice has hints of nutmeg, cinnamon, black pepper and clove. It's used prominently in Bahamian cuisine for souses, soups and dessert fillings. Purchase at your local supermarket or Caribbean markets.

BIRD'S EYE CHILIES: This small chili is very hot (piquant) and spicier than a jalapeño.

BLACK-EYED PEAS: The peas are green when freshly shelled and brown when dried. A narrow black circle is prominent in the center of the bean's belly and is known as the eye. It has a firm and resilient texture when cooked, with a distinct nutty, earthy and savory flavor. Great in rice and soups.

BREADFRUIT: This large tree fruit is bright green and glossy with a rough outer layer. It's a starchy fruit that is similar in taste to potatoes and is edible when baked, fried, boiled or grilled.

BROWNING: A significant ingredient in Bahamian cuisine, it's a blend of caramel color, vegetable concentrates and seasonings. It's used to add a rich flavor and color to rice, soups, stews and gravies.

CALLALOO: This healthy leafy green of the taro root originated from West Africa. It's similar in taste to creamy spinach when cooked, and has a nutty undertone. Enjoy it steamed as a side dish or boiled in soups.

CARIBBEAN CURRY POWDER: Let it be known that no two Caribbean curry powders are the same — each Caribbean island has its own unique way of preparing it. Jamaican curry powder is usually a brighter yellow because more turmeric is added to the spice mixture. Along with its earthy flavors of allspice, there are spicy chili flakes. Curry powders from Guyana, Trinidad and Tobago are usually darker and thicker because more cumin, black peppercorns, nutmeg, cinnamon and cardamom are added. The flavor profile is spicy, earthy and tangy. I prefer to mix both powders for an exceptional tasting Caribbean curry dish.

CARIBBEAN SWEET POTATO: See sweet potato, Caribbean.

CASSAVAS: This long, tapered (shiny brown-skinned) edible starchy tuberous root can be prepared like a potato. It's commonly known as tapioca or yuca, and is a staple vegetable in Bahamian soups as well as cassava bread.

CHADON BENI: A leafy herb that is native to the West Indies. It's similar in taste to cilantro with a slight minty flavor.

COCONUT CREAM: Coconut cream is the first pressing from the coconut. It contains less water, giving it a thicker, more paste-like consistency. It's usually the first part out at the top of a can of coconut milk.

COCONUT JELLY: The jelly is extracted from young coconuts for the famous Gully Wash (gin and coconut water) cocktail or to eat right out of the shell.

COCONUT MILK: It's the thinner milk that follows the coconut cream extracted from the grated meat of a mature coconut. It has a high oil content, most of which is saturated fat. Coconut milk is popular in our curries, stew, rice and desserts.

CONCH: Conch is a species of large edible sea snails. It's a marine gastropod mollusk that is prized for both its edible meat and attractive spiral-shaped shell with a glossy pink or orange interior. They achieve full size at about 3–5 years of age, growing to a maximum of about 12 inches (30 cm) long and weighing about 5 lbs (2.3 kg). Conch has a sweet, slightly smoky flavor similar to abalone or geoduck, with an almost crunchy texture in salads.

CRABAPPLES: Crabapples are wild miniature apples with a sweet and sour flavor profile. They're usually used to make jams.

EDDOES: These small starchy root vegetables are closely related to taro. They're sweet and nutty with a flavor that is more intense than a potato. The skin is inedible and, once cooked, the grayish-white texture is similar to a sweet potato. Eddoes can be eaten mashed or added to soups and stews.

GHEE: Ghee is a class of clarified butter traditionally used in West Indian Cooking.

GREEN ONIONS OR SCALLIONS: Both the white base and green stalks are eaten. The flavor is milder than onions but stronger than chives.

GRITS: Grits are made from corn that is grounded into a coarse meal. They can be purchased in white (ground white corn) or yellow (ground yellow corn), and in a variety of textures. Bahamian native yellow grits are more coarse in texture.

GROUPER: Grouper is a species of fish with lean, succulent meat that has a distinctive-yet-subtle flavor with large flakes and a firm texture. Yellowfin and Gag groupers are found in shallow tropical waters. There are many other varieties since grouper is related to the seabass family.

GUAVAS: This fruit is best adapted to warm

climates. Guava is round, ovoid or pear-shaped and ranges from 2–4 inches (5–10 cm) long. Varieties differ in flavor and seediness. The color of the flesh may be white, pink, yellow or red. The flavor of guavas is creamy with a wonderfully sweet-musky odor. They're great in jams, jellies, sauces and desserts.

GUINEPS: These green drupes are 1–1.5 inches (2.5–4 cm) long and 3/4 inch (2 cm) wide. The pulp is orange or salmon in color with a juicy and pasty texture that is either sweet or sour. Guineps are seasonal and are sold in Caribbean and Asian markets.

HOG PLUMS: These plums are also known as Spanish plums. They are often yellow or purple with a little meat around the seed. Both colors are high in dietary fiber and great as a healthy snack.

JAMAICAN SWEET POTATO, See sweet potato, Jamaican

JUJU: Juju (aka jujube) is an edible oval fruit. The immature fruit is smooth and green with the consistency and taste of an apple, while the mature fruit is brown and wrinkled resembling a small date.

LEMONGRASS: Lemongrass is a tropical island plant in the grass family. It has a sweet lemon-lime taste, with a hint of mint and ginger, and it adds aromatic fragrances to soups and teas. The tough outer stalks should be discarded before dicing or steeping.

LIME LEAVES, SOUR: These leaves have a distinctive lemon-lime flavor that is great to add to Bahamian souse or soups. As an alternative, use kaffir lime leaves available at Asian supermarkets.

MACE: This spice is the aril or net-like sheath that covers the nutmeg seed. It has a fragrant, nutmeg aromatic odor with a warm taste and is used in desserts.

MAGGIE SEASONING: This dark pungent concentrated seasoning sauce is similar in taste to Worcestershire sauce. It's used in soups, stews, sauces and gravies.

MAMEY: This medium to large ovoid fruit has a brown sandpaper but fuzzy peach texture bark. It has a creamy salmon-colored flesh with a large central pit, and a flavor profile of pumpkin, sweet potato, apricots and banana, with notes of vanilla and nutmeg. It's used in shakes, ice cream and other desserts and can be purchased at Caribbean or Latin Supermarkets fresh, canned or in frozen pulp.

MUTTON: Mutton is sheep that is older than 1 year. It's usually harvested at about 3 years old. The meat is red, tough and wonderfully gamy. Mutton is best prepared by braising or steaming in a sauce (Bahamian steam mutton) to tenderize the meat, then spices are used to tone down the gamy flavor. It is available at Caribbean, Asian or Indian markets.

OKRA: Also known as ladies' fingers, okra is valued for its edible green seed pods that can grow to 7 inches (18 cm) in length. Okra is mucilaginous (slimey or gooey), which contributes to the texture of soups or stews. For a less gelatinous texture fry or sauté the okras for about 5 minutes. Okra is available in supermarkets fresh and frozen.

PIGEON PEAS: These peas, also known as Congo peas, are edible when young and green, and are perfect as a healthy snack. Matured seeds are light pale with brown speckles, and should be soaked before cooking. Dried pigeon peas are the main ingredient in Bahamian peas and rice as well as our scrumptious pigeon peas soup.

PLANTAIN: Often referred to as cooking bananas, plantains can be eaten ripe or unripe. Green or pale-yellow plantain flesh is usually bland with a starchy texture; as the fruit ripens the starches are converted to sugar, therefore it can be eaten raw. Green plantains are added to soups or boiled and mashed as a side; ripe yellow plantains are fried as a side. Both types are available in supermarkets.

SAPODILLA: A large berry 1 1/2–3 inches (4–8 cm) in diameter. Its flesh ranges from pale yellow to earthy brown with a grainy-textured skin similar to a well-ripened pear. Sapodilla has an exceptionally sweet and nutty flavor that is great in smoothies, ice cream and other desserts. It's available fresh at Caribbean and Indian markets.

SCALLIONS: See green onions.

SCARLET PLUM: The fruit is an edible oval drupe 1 inch (2.5 cm) long, ripening red (occasionally yellow), and containing a single large seed. The flesh is sweet with a plum-like flavor.

SCOTCH BONNET PEPPERS: This variety of chili pepper is named for its resemblance to a Tam O'Shanter hat. The skin of the pepper has a sweeter flavor but the seeds have good heat that gives a distinctive flavor to jerk spices and many other Caribbean dishes.

SEA GRAPES: A grape-like fruit about 3/4 inch (2 cm) in diameter that ripens to a purplish color. It has a very earthy-sweet flavor that is mainly used to make jams and jellies.

SOUR LIME LEAVES: See lime leaves, sour

SOURSOP: Soursop is a unique heart-shaped, prickly yellowish green fruit. It ranges in size from 4–12 inches (10–30 cm) long and up to 6 inches (15 cm) in width and weighs up to 10–15 lbs (4.5 kg–6.8 kg). Its inner surface is cream colored, fibrous, soft and juicy with hard black seeds that are 1/2–3/4 inch (1–2 cm) long. Soursop (also known as custard apple or guanabana) has a unique acidic yet mellow honeyed flavor profile. Available fresh, or as frozen pulp or nectar in Caribbean and Latin markets.

SUGAR APPLE: The fruit is spherical, 2–4 inches (5–10 cm) in dimension with a thick rind composed of knobby segments. The flesh is fragrant and sweet and resembles the taste of custard, with a color that is creamy white to light yellow.

SUGAR BANANA: Also known as a fig banana, this fruit is about 1 inch (2.5 cm) in diameter and 4 inches (10 cm) long. The banana's skin is thin with a taste that's sweeter than common bananas.

SWEET POTATO, CARIBBEAN: Also known as a boniato, this sweet potato has a dry white flesh and pink-purplish skin with a gentle sweet chestnut flavor.

SWEET POTATO, JAMAICAN: The paler-skin Jamaican sweet potato is not as sweet as the Caribbean sweet potato. The flesh is a pale yellow and has a thin crumbly texture that's similar to a white baking potato.

TAMARIND: This pod-like fruit contains a fleshy, juicy, acidulous pulp that is mature when the flesh is colored brown or reddish brown. The fruit is best described as sweet and sour in taste.

FOR FURTHER *Reading*

Albury, Paul. *The Story of The Bahamas*. MacMillan Caribbean, 1975.

Craton, Michael. *A History of the Bahamas*. San Salvador Press, 1986.

Farnsworth, Paul, and Laurie A. Wilkie. Fish and Grits: Southern, African, and British Influences in Bahamian Foodways. In: H. Regis, ed, *Caribbean and Southern Transitional Perspectives on the U.S. South*

Keegan, William F. *The People Who Discovered Columbus: The Prehistory of the Bahamas*. University Press of Florida, 1992.

Lee, David. (2014, August 5). *British-Inspired Bahamian Dishes* [web log post]. Retrieved from http://hgchristie.com 2014.

INDEX